Worship From Home

Church Without Walls

Canaan Harris

©2020 by Canaan Harris

All Rights Reserved. No parts of this book may be reproduced in any form without written permission from the publisher.

All quotations from the *The Big Book* are from *Alcoholics Anonymous, Fourth Edition* (A.A. World Services, Inc.: New York City, 2001).

Some names and identifying information in this book may have been changed to protect the privacy of individuals.

Cover Design: Canaan Harris
Author photo: Ezekiel Harris

Epangelia Press
3690 Cherry Creek S Dr
Denver, CO 80209
www.worshipfromhome.org

ISBN 978-1-953336-00-2 (*print*)
ISBN 978-1-953336-07-1 (*digital*)

In loving memory of Peggy Dumler

Introduction

Worship From Home is the story of how our church, a 147-year-old mainline congregation in Denver, Colorado, found a new sense of purpose through the coronavirus pandemic. Our experience is so incredible we have to share it, for we believe it might herald a new reformation of the church! Could it be God is using this pandemic to open the door to future opportunities we are only just beginning to imagine?

Not that this hasn't happened before. For instance consider the consequence of the Plague on medieval Europe in the 14th century. Believed to have killed as many as 30-60% of Europe's population, the transformation of socio-economic relationships that followed resulted in the flowering of the Italian Renaissance and the invention of the printing press, providing the social context for the Protestant Reformation.

Consequently, while we grieve the terrible suffering caused by the effects of COVID-19 - including job loss, economic recession, illness and death - as people of faith we trust that the Lord will make a way somehow. And if what our church is now experiencing through doing *Worship From Home* is representative of what's happening elsewhere in the world, it may be that God is preparing us for a major shift in how we use technology similar to what happened 500 years ago.

In fact, from what we've seen, it appears God is using this crisis to teach us a lesson that the church is not a building but a people. For while this concept receives a lot of lip-service, in our experience it wasn't until we were forced to separate from our building under mandated stay-at-home orders that we finally started to understand what it means.

No doubt it helped that, at the same time we had to make this transition as a church from in-person to virtual gatherings, as someone active in the rooms of Alcoholics Anonymous I had a role in my A.A. home-group helping to make the exact same transition. To my surprise, what I discovered is that not only were we able to continue the sacred work of recovery in the virtual space, there were even certain advantages to doing the work in this way.

Being part of such a successful transition in 12-step recovery has encouraged me to think, "Why can't we do the same for the church?" *Worship From Home* and our dream for the potential of a church without walls thus draws on what I've seen to be the proven success of the online rooms of A.A. to provide an authentic, effective communal spiritual experience in a virtual space.

Even now, we are learning about the virtual room and how we relate to one another in it at exponential speed because we are having to adapt to it so quickly. Considering all that has come to light through this experience already it's like our whole society is taking a look in the mirror - seeing what for too long we've tried to ignore - so that somehow this pandemic is forcing everyone to face some hard truths.

In the process, we are making needed changes, personally, institutionally, and systemically, that if we can be honest with ourselves we know have been a long time coming. Personally I choose to believe that all of this is part of God's plan and purpose. Could it be that reality is actually God's will for us? For as the scripture says, "We know that all things work together for good for those that love God and are called according to God's purpose" (Romans 8:28).

I'm not saying God created the coronavirus, not by any means, however we are already seeing how God is taking this pandemic and using it to break down the walls of separation that divide people here and around the world, even as it opens up new opportunities to share the gospel.

Those of us participating in *Worship From Home* on Sundays as well as the other offerings the church provides find that we maintain a tremendous advantage over those who are not connecting in this way. For by doing church online we are finding a way to participate in the Body of Christ and the Family of God without allowing ourselves to become defeated by circumstances beyond our control.

God promises, "Behold, I am doing a new thing; now it springs forth, do you not perceive it? I will make a way in the wilderness and rivers in the desert" (Isaiah 43:19). Could this mean that God is using this very pandemic as a way to create new ways for the church to be connected beyond the walls of our building, or even, as Jesus taught, to help provide fresh wineskins for the new wine, because otherwise the old wineskins would burst (see Mark 2:18-22)?

By this analogy, technology is not the enemy of the church. Instead, I believe God inspires technology - Zuckerberg's invention in 2004, for instance - the same as God inspired Gutenberg's invention in 1440. Indeed, God will continue to provide the means by which the people of God can stay connected, even when circumstances like pandemic and stay-at-home orders threaten to keep us apart. For as Jesus said: "With God, all things are possible" (Matthew 19:26).

I believe it, too, for with the numbers of what we're seeing today the truth is I've never been so involved in evangelism in my life as I have these past few months, simply as the result of doing *Worship From Home*. Our members are happy as well. For instance, when I told one of our church's best supporters how many more people we are reaching now that we've moved beyond the walls of the church he responded, "Isn't that what we're supposed to be doing? Sharing the message with all the nations?" (Matthew 28:19).

So from my perspective, God's hand is clearly in this. And actually, looking back it's nothing short of a miracle how certain pieces fell into place to allow us to catch the wind of this movement we call *Worship From Home*. Signs like these are why we are even now daring to believe that what we are experiencing is in fact a reformation of the larger church similar to what happened in 1517 when Martin Luther first invited people to interpret the Bible for themselves.

For despite everyone's worries about closing the church, in our experience closing the building only strengthened the actual church. That's because by figuring out how to let go of our idolatry of the building, we are finally learning what it means not just to "go" to church but to "be" the church.

Jesus said, "Go ye therefore and make disciples" (Matthew 28:18-20), not "Go sit inside a building Sundays at 10am". That's why, as pastor of a church that is now experiencing this miraculous revival of *Worship From Home*, I trust that God is calling us - all of us - to be the church without walls.

1

When are we going back to church? As pastor of a traditional big-steeple metropolitan church, I probably hear that question as often as any other these days. In fact, just the other day I was talking with one of our members who's become very connected online, yet she still worries about when we are "going back" to church.

Of course I empathize, for I understand how she misses the church sanctuary and gathering with her friends. However to me it was striking how this lady called to ask me about "going back" to church while at that very instant I watched as our church clocked 15,000 likes on our Facebook page.

For in that moment it hit me like a bolt of lightning that the church is something more than just our 750 seat sanctuary currently standing empty in our building on Cherry Creek. Indeed, it was becoming hard to ignore the fact that our church was already more active in the virtual space than we ever had been in our physical space before the pandemic. What I realized is that our church had already grown from less than 500 followers on Facebook to what at that point was 15,000 followers affiliating by liking our page.

That's how suddenly, in a way that never happened before, I finally got it that the church is not a building. Or in other words, it became clear to me how going to church doesn't make someone a Christian anymore than going to a garage makes someone a car. It's something I thought I understood - something I've believed and professed all my years of ministry - but, somehow, for the first time, I really got it.

Because what I recognized is that 15,000 people could never gather in that physical space at one time, whereas in the virtual space everyone can gather simultaneously, and there's room for unlimited numbers! For while prior to COVID-19, I saw filling our 750 seat sanctuary as the outside limit to participation, now - in just four months time - it's become clear that our 750 seat sanctuary is not nearly large enough to hold the virtual congregation. So it puts it in perspective that we can be church in the virtual room in ways we could never before imagine in the physical room.

There's a meme going around social media right now titled "The Current State of Things" in which a pastor complains how "I'm going to 26 meetings a week to try and figure out how to have in-person church," whereas the people say "We're watching church on the couch, wearing pajamas and drinking coffee, plus we can mute you. So we're good".

Speaking as a pastor, it seems the point of this meme is that, with all our concern about going back to church, the fact is that for a lot of people it seems we are doing just fine right now worshiping God from home. In truth, it may be that we're doing better than we've otherwise done in a long time. For one thing, we are now being forced to figure out what it means to "be" church as a result of the fact that we can no longer "go" to church as a matter of routine, which in my experience had become more than a little bit stale.

Again, no doubt we've all heard the phrase "the church is not a building" before. Yet still we make an idol of the building, and all our talk about "going to" church instead of being the church only illustrates our idolatry. For typically what we mean by "going to" church is attending a worship service in a church building on Sunday morning: a building that costs many tens of thousands of dollars to heat and cool and maintain just so people like ourselves can come inside and sit down in an uncomfortable pew for an hour.

Obviously, this isn't something the average pew sitter ever thinks about. But from my perspective as the career pastor of a denominational church, I can say without exaggeration that for each man, woman and child in attendance it costs a church like ours at least $1000 or more a year just to heat and cool and clean and maintain the building. This is not unusual for our area. Consider, for instance, a church that budgets $200K annually on facilities maintenance to serve a 200 person average worship attendance. All churches' building costs aren't that high, but some are even higher.

Sound the alarm, but from my experience it is typical for churches like ours to dip deep into our pockets to prop up what is far too much building for such a little group. Where do we get the money? In our case, it's mostly from returns on our investments. And of course we are grateful for the faithful contributions of our people and the generations that have gone before that have brought us to this time and place, by the grace of God. However the writing has been on the wall for years now that this pattern is unsustainable.

Also, as we've all heard it said, "Sunday morning at 10am is the most segregated hour in America". And while there are all kinds of reasons, both good and bad, why we align with others like ourselves in our religious communities, the fact is that many churches are extremely homogeneous in their membership. A lot of this has to do with the neighborhood in which the building resides: whether that area is seen as welcoming to people from diverse backgrounds; or if it's on a convenient bus-line; or whether there's adequate parking; all of which must be negotiated before meeting the people.

In contrast, during this time of pandemic, it's as if all of those factors of cost and geography and transportation have been suspended at least for a moment. As a result, our church community has found the joy of worshiping conveniently from home while connecting and evangelizing like what we've never done before. What's more, today thousands of people are connecting together online, not only in our neighborhood, but across the country, and around the world. So after years of thinking of the church as centering around what happens at our building on Cherry Creek, it is truly exhilarating to be reaching so many more people with the message of Jesus Christ.

In fact, I've never seen such a season of evangelism and revival before! And what we've discovered is that prior to this pandemic we were, in effect, hiding behind our walls waiting on people to come to us. Whereas now, the church has no choice but to try and meet people where they are, which in this time of social-distancing has been online.

In that respect, when you compare the way we are doing ministry now with how the ministry operated before the pandemic, we as the church have identified the log in our eye and it's our concern around the building (Matthew 7:5). Because for too long the building has been more of a focus of our attention than it is a container for a greater mission. Not that we ever intended to make an idol of it, only that in a 147-year-old church - with a building that's far larger and that needs far more attention than our over-taxed volunteer group can prioritize - the building ends up becoming an end in itself rather than a vehicle for carrying the message.

Sadly, this mentality can become a vicious cycle where, as I've often experienced it, almost as soon as newcomers walk in the doors certain old-timers will inevitably try and chase them away - subconsciously or otherwise - almost as if they are worried that their own status will diminish if the organization becomes any larger. Consequently, what I've learned is that, over time, our pattern of "going to" church can easily become an idolatry of not only the building but also of the current and former occupants of that building!

That's why the old established go-to-church-in-the-building style of church has been in decline for a long time, and why the older the church typically the worse the decline. Why? Because that's what happens when a church is no longer built around work happening right now, and instead is built around some kind of legacy, reminiscing on some nostalgic time that may in actual fact have never been. For sad to say, but whenever we preserve a building and style of worship exactly like it was in order to memorialize days gone by, it becomes an idol to ourselves and not a way to honor God.

Not that we haven't tried to take on projects of evangelism. For instance, we have a very active group at Central that is always encouraging us to go knocking on doors or putting up signs inviting people to church and if not for their efforts we would have never started broadcasting on Facebook Live a couple of years ago. For the fact is, over the past several years we have done everything we possibly could to try and push the ball forward on evangelism, something that just wasn't a priority of the previous generation, and if it was not for the steps we had already taken we'd never have been in a position to catch the wave of this new era.

Regardless, whatever efforts we make in commemorating the past won't help us to encourage new people in joining. For as I've oftentimes had to remind people in the pews, if the true purpose of a church is to look to a brighter hope of the future (see Revelation 22:12) then why would anyone new want to be part of an organization that places so much emphasis on idolizing a past they were never a part of?

Recall how God speaks through the prophet Amos, saying, "I hate, I despise your festivals! I cannot stand the stench of your solemn assemblies" (Amos 5:21). Could this critique apply to what's become of the institutional church today because of our habit of making an idol of our accumulated resources and hoarding them for our own exclusive use?

So from what I can tell, the model of church as institution has already outlived its purpose. In some cases it has even become something opposite of what it was intended to be. Meaning that perhaps the church as institution is producing the very opposite kind of widgets than God created it to do. And if that is the case, maybe it's time to look to a different model of church or at least try doing something different.

Again, don't shoot the messenger, but I believe the project of the church as we had it before is utterly unsustainable. Just the cost of keeping our message behind closed doors is extraordinary and puts a huge burden on contributions and income from investments (for those fortunate to have them) that could potentially be used elsewhere, especially when the emphasis shifts to the virtual space. What's more, not only is the old model costly, it's more or less totally ineffective, at least compared to what we are seeing today where we are literally reaching hundreds of times as many people as before, and that after only a few months time.

Before the pandemic, for instance, we would often worship Sunday mornings with no more than 200 people attending in-person, although our sanctuary seats 750. Yet even going back to the glory days of our history, people boast of how they can remember having several hundred in attendance on Sunday mornings, and of course those memories are typically far more grandiose in retrospect than in reality.

In contrast, by doing *Worship From Home* our church has exploded from a couple hundred in-person to now tens-of-thousands tuning-in online each week. This means that we are now doing worship with thousands of people rather than gathering as a few people waiting behind our walls and somehow expecting people to come in. Ultimately, it's made me realize that whatever we were doing before by spending all our effort to keep the building open when all along we had the capacity to share the message with so many more people was actually idolatrous in a certain way.

That's the big lesson here for me. For after this experience of *Worship From Home* I've come to believe what we were doing before was actually making an idol of the building. Even worse, I believe we were making an idol of ourselves by directing all of these resources - thousands of dollars per person per year - to speak to a small group of people just like ourselves, rather than to do what Jesus commanded us to do which is to share the gospel with all the nations.

Not that these are new conclusions: we've known for a long time that the project was unsustainable. Rather the reason I can finally say all these things out loud is because I can now see a way forward, whereas in the past I felt like I had an obligation to keep doing things the way we've always done.

As a result, I have to admit there's a part of me that goes along kicking and screaming into this uncertain future, because as an ordained clergy-person I've made my living for the past twenty-five years by drawing income from my work at the church. Also I've done the same Saturday sermon writing/Sunday worship routine for as long as I can remember, so I guess you might say old habits die hard. But the fact is, God's been working on me, though the trials of these past couple of years in particular. Looking back on these challenges, I imagine that if it was not for what we've already been through we would never have found the freedom from constraint on our church that has allowed us to remain open to whatever future God has in store for us.

So in contrast to all those who are wishing to "go back" to the way things were, because of my tremendously positive experience in transitioning from in-person spiritual work to virtual spiritual work both in church and in the rooms of recovery, I already see the silver lining of this new style. For not only do we benefit by not having to spend all our time and energy maintaining a building, and allowing the leadership to focus on other areas besides fussing over the needs of our physical plant, we are helping more people have better access to our message and other resources of the ministry since it no longer costs people - in travel time or gas money, for instance - to be a part of the church.

What's more, and speaking only anecdotally of course, what I've discovered by sitting in the Zoom rooms of Alcoholics Anonymous every day for the past 4 months is that virtual meetings are as capable as in-person meetings of passing on the principles of the program. Even better, it seems that virtual communication may even potentially allow more intimacy in communication because often people find it easier to share their authentic thoughts and feelings from behind a screen than in a room full of people.

Finally, and most importantly, there's no question in my mind that by reaching out and using the best technology available to share the message with people out there in the world far better fulfills The Great Commission - to "Go and make disciples of all nations" (Matthew 28:16-20) - than whatever we were doing before. For although our previous style of worship was certainly sincere, now I wonder why we ever really expected other people to come inside.

Worship From Home is thus a new reformation of the church because it convicts us of our selfishness in keeping all of God's good gifts for the exclusive use of the club that meets in our building. Forced by stay-at-home orders to venture beyond our walls, we are now learning to follow Jesus' command to go out into the highways and byways, indeed into all the world, to bring everyone to the banquet (Luke 14:23). For now that we are reaching out to meet folks where they are, we are finally discovering the truth of the matter that the church is not a building, but a people.

2

Of course, in order to tell the story of what became *Worship From Home*, it requires me to start from a particular vantage point so that I can best describe what was going on back when we first started along this journey. For while in approaching this story I could go back to almost any point in time, at the very least I should return to the events of about two years ago, when we first had to deal with some very difficult hardship in the life of the church. So much so it took having a harvest, or a refining fire in the church, in order to resolve the situation (see Psalm 66:10).

In fact, perhaps it would be best if I went back to a day around three years ago, in the late spring/early summer of 2017, when I got a mysterious call from a man I'll refer to as "the prophet," a man I'd heard of before but had never met, the pastor of a big church in Texas. The prophet, who herein will remain nameless, called to tell how they had been seeing signs and wonders and been given prophecies that spoke about me and about the church in Denver.

He then told me that he wasn't sure what it was all about but the message was very clear and it said "Hold your seat!" "Hold your seat!": this was the prophecy given specifically for me as the pastor of the church. And at the time, I wasn't sure how to interpret it, but that's how I'll start this story.

Because as I said, I could start this story almost anywhere. For instance, going back to when I was a boy, I could talk about growing up in Georgia where my great-uncles were popular Southern Baptist preachers and evangelists. We were literally immersed in this culture back in the days when revival meetings were still the main event of summer. Remember crowding in the back of the church to hear the fiery preachers? Singing shaped-note hymns a cappella led by a song-leader keeping time on his knee? Or eating fried chicken and watermelon under a canopy of magnolia trees?

That's the world I grew up in, and really it's why I became a preacher, because I believed in the promise that one day there would be another revival in this world and I wanted to be a part of it. In fact, on June 1st, I celebrated my 25th Anniversary of serving full-time in congregational ministry. Hard to believe from when I started as the pastor of that little white-steepled church in

River View, Alabama all those many years ago that we would be in this situation today.

My path was fairly traditional in that I attended seminary in my early 20's, where I met my wife, Niki, then served churches in Texas, Tennessee, Kentucky, and Connecticut before I started as Associate Pastor at Central, Denver in 2007. In 2012 I became Senior Pastor, and there's no question that today I have quite a privileged position as the leader of an established, affluent church in a vibrant city.

Over the years, we've experienced modest growth here at Central, which for a denominational church like ours is so rare that even the meagre success we found of maybe 15 baptisms a year put us in the top ten-percent for growth of churches of our brand, the Disciples of Christ, here in the United States. And in my experience, working to revitalize an old established church is very hard work: it feels like you are trying to resurrect a dinosaur. So while even at the time I recognized that these were not quite the fruits of ministry I had hoped for and that I believed were possible, the truth is I allowed those modest successes to satisfy me and I was content with those results and with my position.

So I'll say it again, even as I share this history, I can't help but to be reminded that as a career professional pastor I do have a particular vested interest in the institutional model of the church. In fact, I imagine I could have been content to stay in that position, serving an affluent church enjoying modest growth, for the remainder of my career in ministry.

Then, out of the clear blue, I received this mysterious call from the man I later learned was a prophet. Again, the call was totally unexpected, the prophet said he didn't know me either, but in their experience of signs and wonders his church had been given my name and our church's name directly from God with the message that I was to "hold my seat". "So what does this mean?" I asked him, but he said he had "no other information" to give me "at this time".

Meanwhile, the church continued our cycle of growth throughout 2017. For example, that October, I accompanied a group of adults on a mission trip to Thailand, our first international trip, while our youth planned a mission to Honduras in 2018. In those days, we had been in this pattern of moderate growth for so many years that I just assumed it would continue.

Then the bottom fell out of everything. In March of 2018, we discovered an ugly conspiracy to destroy our church leadership through a slander and defamation campaign. That's a story for another day, but somehow God led us through these very difficult trials that ultimately made us stronger as individuals and as a church. For only by going through the refining fire could our eyes finally be opened to discern the true from the false.

And although we suffered extraordinary disappointment, in retrospect we recognize that what we went through was a harvest that allowed God to separate the wheat from the chaff (see Matthew 3:12).

For while ultimately our leadership was vindicated, in the process we lost around half of our in-person participants. Spiritually, I was reminded of the story of Gideon in his campaign against the Midianites (Judges 7:5). Recall how Gideon started with 300,000 men and was worried that was not enough, but God reduced his army down to just 300 men before conquering the Midianites. For not only did God want to purify the group and see which ones were true before the conquest of the new land, but also to prove that the victory was from God and not from human origin.

Thanks be to God for our strong Spirit-filled leaders that remained faithful throughout this season of harvest! One leader spoke to the quality of character required of us during this time when he said, "What it comes down to is that I have to look at myself in the mirror every morning". Of course that's true, but at the time I had no idea how rare it is for a person to have this kind of courage and integrity.

Yet the fact is everyone who remained, every single person, was tested in the fire like the three Hebrew children and found worthy (see Daniel 3:19-25). That's God's plan for the church, that the faithful will be purified from vessels of clay to become vessels of silver and gold (see 2 Timothy 2:20-21). For after this season of harvest, all that we went though in discerning the true from the false, the people who remain in the church today are the most faithful, trustworthy, and integral people I know. In fact, I have a lot of clergy friends and I know only one other pastor with as much trust and confidence in his church as I have in the people of Central.

So we thank God for the faithful remnant (Romans 11:5). For at times, the persecution we faced was so difficult that even I questioned whether to put down the fight. For instance, our Moderator, Peggy Dumler, came under the most hateful campaign of defamation I've ever seen conducted against a volunteer. Yet we were steeled to the task by the love of our friends, and I held fast to the message of the prophet who had asked me to "hold my seat". For in those days, I would reach out to him and to a few other colleagues regularly for encouragement. And the prophet told me still more of what he knew, so as to strengthen me for the hard road ahead.

Consequently, after defending our church from the most immediate harm, we took every possible step to protect ourselves from this ever happening again. And in the final analysis, it all helped us to become the people we are today. For example, the challenges of 2018 forced us to create legal protections to defend ourselves from attacks on our business model that we hadn't otherwise prepared for, as well as to streamline our organizational structure so that we could be equipped for taking on the work we are now dealing with today. Because, if you don't know, churches are notoriously *laissez-faire* when it comes to volunteers - they call it the "any warm butt in a seat" syndrome - which unfortunately can foster a system where a group of church bullies has inordinate sway over the way a church is run.

Accordingly, we made changes to our bylaws limiting who had authority to participate in elections and voted these changes into our governing documents so that people could no longer threaten to use their legacy membership status to hijack our decision-making process. Little did we know while making these official policy changes around who is eligible to vote that only a few months later Peggy would be gone and we would need to hold our first mail-in election in our 147 year history! For without these changes proscribing voting eligibility, our church might have been subject to hostile takeover from the very disaffected members that were trying to destroy the church over the past two years.

In addition, having suffered some break-ins and property damage as a result of the conflict, we took measures to secure the building with online cameras, lock-bars on the exterior doors and other measures we didn't have before to allow us to keep tabs on our 60,000 square-foot facility remotely so we can be confident everything is secure. We also made other changes during this time such as replacing our bookkeeping, custodial and maintenance staff with contractors that we could more easily manage remotely.

What's more, a couple of years ago we began broadcasting our Sunday services on Facebook Live, although we were only getting 100 or less views on average. All this is to say that we had already established an infrastructure around broadcasting video messages. That's how, when the stay-at-home orders were issued, we were able to pivot so quickly in order to try and follow God's lead by doing a new thing.

Again, I believe if it were not for the season of antagonism that began in 2018 there's no way our church would have been prepared to roll with the changes that came with this pandemic. Most importantly, before we faced these ugly events in our church I was perfectly content to be a success story of the institutional model, so I can only imagine that I would have had a much harder time letting that go if our journey had only continued along that upwards trajectory. For without that disappointment, no doubt it would have been far more difficult to let go of the old style of "going to church," whereas instead we seemed to be able to transition without a lot of friction, which is why we are now able to "be the church" by meeting people where they are.

So I give all the credit to Peggy Dumler for forcing these issues around security, maintenance, changes to bylaws, and making sure we were technologically up-to-date.

Often I would ask her why she was driving everything so hard to completion. "What are you worried about?" I'd ask. "Don't we have enough time?" And Peggy would respond with a football analogy, saying she wanted to take care of all questions of defense so that when she was finished with her term of service the church could finally go on the offense.

It was a hard couple of years, but in retrospect there's no doubt that if it was not for having to protect against these attacks on our church in 2018, we would never have been prepared to take on the tasks required of us in 2020. For in the final analysis, the end result of the challenges of the past was that they steeled the core group of leaders to the task. Thus this season of antagonism became a refining fire for all the faithful members who ultimately stood together to help defend the church throughout these difficult times. So the fact that we were able to move into this new style without any more encumbrance is really evidence that God was with us through all the trials that led us to this point.

Looking back, one moment in particular from this season became for me a flash-point for all the lessons we learned during this time. For as I mentioned, the youth group had been planning a mission trip to Honduras in the summer of 2018. Because I had taken the adults to Thailand in 2017 I was not planning to accompany the youth to Honduras. But since we had lost a number of our adult sponsors and other participants as a result of conflict in the church, I decided I would go on the mission trip to Honduras after all.

And it was there, in a poor street children's church in the *barrio* of Suyapa, in the state of Yoro, that I had one of the most profound spiritual experiences of my life. For there, on the wall of the modest room where they gathered, the children had painted a picture of the Great White Throne (see Revelation 20:11). And on the final evening of our worship, the pastor called me up to the front where he had me get down on my knees before the Throne. Then he asked all the street children to come forward and lay their hands on me to pray for me and for my ministry.

So there I was, knelt down on the floor of that little street church, feeling the imprint of dozens of children's hands laid on me in prayer, and hearing the voices of dozens of children speaking in a language I barely understand, all shouting out prayers to God to bless me and my ministry. And in that moment I realized that this was exactly where I needed to be: that despite all the hurt and disappointment we were experiencing at that time, and little did we know it was only the beginning of a long season of antagonism, if it were not for the challenges we were facing I would never have been in a position to receive this tremendous blessing!

That realization hit me like a slap in the face, and in that moment it made me consider for the first time whether this terrible thing that had happened in the church that hurt so many people and divided the congregation might in fact be God's will for us. For if it was in fact true, as I experienced it, that when the children laid their hands on me in prayer in Suyapa I was exactly where I was supposed to be, then it follows that whatever happened at the church that caused me to be on that mission trip to Honduras when otherwise I wouldn't be must have been in God's plan and purpose!

This was such a revelation for me, because up to that point I had been so angry about what was truly a terrible betrayal of people's roles and responsibilities in the church that led to the division and strife we were experiencing. However what happened in Honduras was so convincing that I was, for the first time, forced to reconsider whether or not the hardship we were facing in the church was a good thing or a bad thing, which in itself was a significant step towards beginning to see how God is at work through all of this.

What's more, I recall coming back to church and telling that story from the pulpit, of how my experience of the children of Suyapa laying hands on me and praying convinced me that I was right where I was supposed to be. Afterwards, I will never forget how one trusted Elder came up to me in the receiving line and asked, "Do you really believe that? That what happened in Honduras means everything's going to be okay?" It was my friend Jim, someone I respect very much. So I said, "Yes, I do,

Jim, the experience was just so real it was like God was speaking directly to me". "Well then," he said, "if you really believe that things will get better how about acting as if things are better already? For it sounds like God is telling you that it's all under control".

I will never forget that conversation. Because it was then that I was finally able to employ a spiritual tool that I had never had much success with until then, which is to act "as if" something was already true, even in the face of what appears to be evidence to the contrary. It's like the recovery aphorism that defines "fear" as "False Evidence Appearing Real". For it is in lessons like these that we are able to gain discernment, where we learn to distinguish true from false.

Again, if it were not for the battles we went through as a church family the past two years we would likely not have been equipped to face the challenges of today under the coronavirus pandemic. Because when we first heard about COVID-19 and discovered that we had to close the church building overnight, the fact is that Peggy, the other leaders, and I were able to move relatively quickly. We heard about the order to close on Friday, March 13 and we had *Worship From Home* up and running March 15th. Yet it might never have happened if not for the steps we had already taken to assure that everything was locked down and under control.

That's why throughout all of the ups-and-downs of ministry and through the various trials, perhaps more than anything I can now see how God has been positioning me to roll with the punches, take things one day at a time, and to open my mouth and trust that God will give me the words to speak. It's been a hard road with some hard lessons and a lot of disappointments and frustrated expectations, but what I've learned has been invaluable. Which is to trust in the Lord; that God is always working for me, not against me; and that every challenge presents an opportunity. Also, I've learned to be more discerning and to not take things so personally.

But most importantly, I've learned to give thanks to God in all things, because somehow or another what we learned from these terrible trials over the past two years forced us to get ready for whatever came next. And because we had spent the past two years getting our house in order, when COVID-19 hit we were free to concentrate our attention on the present and not worry about the past, thus allowing us to catch the wave of this new reformation of the church.

3

Regardless of the gravity of what is happening with *Worship From Home*, there's a reason I wanted to share it as a memoir, for it seems like the kind of story that can tell itself. But as I shared in the introduction there's another story I need to tell, adjacent to this one, which also needs to be woven into the fabric of the narrative.

After everything we went through, our team was leaner, stronger, and more trusting. The trials of the past two years had forged a level of friendship with one another that can only be experienced by going through the fire together. And for my part, I discovered the advantage of finding a new perspective that allows me to know that God will give me whatever I might need - whatever strength is necessary - to meet the challenges of each day. Gaining this perspective was something very hard won; but now that I've learned to think this way I have found a tremendous sense of peace about facing life's circumstances, whatever they might be.

Fast-forward to December 2019, which is when I first had a premonition of sorts that something was about to change, even suggesting to our trustees we might want to move our investments into more conservative funds. Others shared the same concerns. So it was that, effective February 3, at the very peak of the market, we took half our total stock investments and sheltered them in the most conservative funds available, keeping the other half in a more aggressive portfolio. From the time we requested the change to when the transfer was effected took about six weeks, so it was good we gave the order when we did, because if we had waited until the downturn it would have been too late.

In the meantime, we were hearing rumors out of China about the novel coronavirus, but because the news is always so politicized and partisan it was difficult to discern the true from the false. Plus all of us had a lot on our plate just in the normal work of the church and in the routines we had established with our families and the other things that balanced out our lives. So the fact is, I wasn't paying as close attention to what was going on as I could have been.

By late February, we heard more rumors of the pandemic but I tried not to worry. That is until Monday, February 27 when I sat down with a friend - a very well-informed, well-travelled, wealthy man whom I'm not at liberty to name. Recently, he'd concluded working on a political campaign where he was traveling all over the country for months, and as a result he was very knowledgeable and up-to-date. We had coffee at The Market on Larimer Square, a local landmark. My friend lived in that area - so I parked and we walked from near his apartment. Ironically this same place would be one of the first announced to close permanently during the economic shut down of early COVID-19.

Ostensibly, the reason we were having coffee that day was to talk about his experience on the campaign trail. That is until he told me he was about to get on an emergency flight that afternoon to go back to Boston where he maintains his primary residence. He shared with me an email from a friend of his - an expert in a position to know things - who said there would be travel bans and shut downs and that, if he didn't want to be separated from his family back East, he needed to get out of Denver at the first opportunity.

In any case, this conversation with a friend was the first I'd heard of anyone taking the coronavirus so seriously. And because he is somebody I trust and respect, I remember leaving that conversation, going back to my office, and immediately ordering 50 n-95 masks on eBay! I was able to secure them for about $.50 a mask, or about $20 for the whole lot, so I felt like I was adequately preparing myself.

The following day, however, I got a message from the eBay seller apologizing because they were all out of masks. So after looking online and seeing how these masks were now no longer available, I finally started to take the threat more seriously. At that point we stocked up on certain groceries filling our freezer and gathering paper goods. However, looking back I can remember picking up my son from school and going to the gym as late as Tuesday, March 10, just before stay-at-home orders were issued in Colorado.

In fact, we would have gone to the gym that Thursday, March 12, on our regular routine but I remember Ezekiel had a cold and so I said to him, "Okay, we can stay home from the gym today, but we will have to go back tomorrow, or as soon as you feel better". Then of course it was the very next day that the governor issued stay at home orders for Colorado and all gym facilities were ordered to close.

So we were caught totally off guard, although in retrospect if I had thought about what these signs meant, along with all the other things being revealed, I probably should have guessed that something like this would happen. For as I recall, Peggy was far more attuned to these things than I was. She had gotten sick with a very bad cough for quite a long time, maybe six weeks, back in December through mid-January, so she wondered if she might have had some early exposure to this virus, and I remember her sounding the alarm about these things long before the world noticed.

That's why for two Sundays prior to stay-at-home orders being announced I was preaching sermons detailing what I thought would be the new protocol for social-distancing. Under the circumstances, I just expected to prepare for heavily modified in-person services because at that time we would never have guessed that we would not be going back to in-person services for another 4 months and counting.

For example, preparing for what I assumed would be the new protocol, earlier on that same week the orders were to be announced I had gone out and bought several thousand prepackaged alcohol wipes for people to use to wipe their hands, because we expected we would still be holding in-person church, only with restrictions. Thursday, March 12, I wrote a letter to the congregation detailing the various social-distancing measures that we were expecting to put in place at our service that coming Sunday. On Friday the Governor's mandated stay-at-home orders came out, so we had to change our plan.

None of us could ever have expected just how abruptly the stay-at-home orders would take effect, so when it came to a head everyone just had to shift immediately. In fact, it was not until Saturday, March 14th that we finally announced the decision not to worship at the church. We weren't quite sure what we should do instead, but because we had been broadcasting our service live on Facebook from the sanctuary for around two years already, we thought we'd just continue that broadcast Sunday mornings as well as try and connect people on Zoom for small-group fellowship.

Furthermore, after Niki and I prayed over it, we made the decision kind of on-the-fly to broadcast our worship service from home rather than from the church sanctuary, which was what a lot of our clergy friends seemed to be doing. Our rationale was that since everybody else was stuck at home just like we were, to do this from our living room was more authentic and relatable than trying to replicate our service in the sanctuary. Also I decided it would be better for us to have a conversation between us rather than to present a formal sermon-type message. We've done this type of conversation style message before on occasion so I imagined it would come across as the most organic style of communication, plus I thought Niki and I talking together would be more relatable than just me having a monologue.

We spent Saturday announcing our change in plans to everyone by every means we had available - phone, email, Facebook, and group texts - then I spent the rest of my time that Saturday figuring out Zoom. Zoom was a brand-new technology to me, but I felt it was important to offer it so that we could continue to connect in small groups and our goal was to make that happen that very next day so that we could move forward without any break in our services.

But actually that's where this story of *Worship From Home* best intersects with what I believe is the parallel story that made such an impact on our project. Because the first time I ever heard of Zoom is from a young man I'll call K. who asked me that day to help him start a Zoom meeting to be modeled on the format of the 7am Attitude Adjustment.

For if you don't know, the 7am Attitude Adjustment is a famous meeting of Alcoholics Anonymous that traditionally meets at what we call the York Street Meeting House in Denver on the corner of 13th and York Streets. We call it Attitude Adjustment because of the aphorism that explains, in regards to the question in the Serenity Prayer of the things you can change and the things you cannot change, that "the only thing you can change is your attitude". One of the great blessings of my life is that I've been attending this meeting since I moved here in 2007, and for about 10 years now I've gone almost every morning, 7 days a week.

Because for me, being part of a recovery community has a tremendous impact on my mental health, especially as a clergy person. For as the saying goes, "A.A. is where priests learn from plumbers how to live". So if it were not for having found my seat in the rooms now for the past 21 years and counting, I cannot imagine where I would be today.

However, before I get started talking about my involvement in A.A. I should probably first address the elephant in the room which is the principle of anonymity A.A. is founded upon. Specifically, the Traditions would want me to clarify that A.A. has no connection with my message because they are committed not to be allied with any sectarian religion (Tradition 10). What's more, some A.A.'s might take issue with me for even mentioning my involvement in the program because of their strict interpretation of Tradition 11, which states that "we need always maintain personal anonymity at the level of press, radio and film".

Such strict interpretation of this Tradition is changing these days, however, especially in the era of social-media with people sharing their sobriety milestones on Facebook, and with online rooms and pages like Remote Recovery where most everyone participates using their full names. Likewise in the Zoom rooms, while some people would rather join with a blank screen and an anonymous moniker, others like me use my full name and connect via a live video screen.

So while I value the principle of anonymity and practice it in my day-to-day affairs, after some fear and trembling I've decided to share about being a part of A.A. as part of the narrative of this memoir. That's because this story is about my experience with connecting to real spiritual community and sacred life during this time of social-distancing, and my participation in A.A. has been a necessary and essential part of that journey.

The bottom line is that I go to a meeting every day because it is the cornerstone of my devotional life and practice. So while some might disagree, I try to balance the principle of anonymity (Tradition 11) with A.A.'s primary purpose (Tradition 5), which is "to share the message" with those who still suffer. Consequently, while I have chosen to tell my story, at the same time I pray I've been respectful of others' anonymity by not naming anyone else in the rooms.

That being said, Friday, March 13th, I spoke up at the 7am Attitude Adjustment, sharing how, as important as it was for me to be in the rooms, because of my responsibility to the people I care about at home I'm not coming back until we figure this stuff out. Afterwards K. called me to say he was feeling the same and asked if I would be willing to help him to replicate the Attitude Adjustment format on Zoom.

So it was that Saturday we connected - just the two of us - and had our first conversation on Zoom, the prototype of the meeting we are having to this day. And because it was just the two of us, that first session wasn't really a meeting per se, for while we started off following the format, after about half an hour we sidetracked into other conversations. Still my friend K. was always quick to check us whenever we went off topic saying, "This isn't in the appropriate format". Again, this was K.'s project to try and replicate the meeting online, I was just happy to be along for the ride!

We met that first morning for the test, then afterwards we both sent out private invitations with the Zoom link to friends. The next morning we had 12 people online that we would likely have otherwise seen at the in-person Attitude Adjustment meeting. Around 25 people joined us the next day, then 50 the next, until the point where there's now as many as 160 people on that meeting every morning at 7am.

Over the same time, we watched as attendance at the clubs dwindled down from our usual 80-100 or more at the 7am to just 10 or less, and this was before they were mandated to close. For at the height of the stay-at-home orders here in Denver, even the A.A. clubhouses had to close for several weeks. Eventually they opened back up to groups of ten people or less. However, here we are in the middle of July and still only a handful of people - maybe a dozen or so - are meeting in person, while about 120 are still meeting online. As a result, we have committed to continuing the online option until clubs open back up with no restrictions.

It's truly a blessing, and what's more I've discovered that attending the online meeting every day has the same impact on my thinking that going to the physical space all these years did, and I think that's the point.

For after fifteen weeks of meeting virtually rather than physically I can now safely say from experience that I've had the same program satisfied through the virtual space that I had by taking part in a meeting in the physical space. Even better, some people open up more intimately on the virtual meeting than they would in the physical meeting. For instance, certain friends I've known a long time but rarely hear speak are now sharing more deeply in the virtual space because they're not having to do that in a room full of actual people.

Probably one of the reasons the 7am Attitude Adjustment was able to make this transition from in-person to virtual meetings so readily is because we use a standard format that seems to have adapted well to Zoom meetings. For if you don't know, a common format for 12-step meetings is modeled after the Quaker meeting style in which there is no program other than inviting people to take turns to speak on a topic selected for the day. Using this format, we maintain a strict policy that says people must share in the solution, which means that we have to talk about how the program has helped us to find an "attitude adjustment".

Also, because our meeting is so large, we limit sharing to three minutes or less in order to allow everyone the opportunity to participate. So it seems that this in-person format has adapted to Zoom technology primarily because it allows each person to have an equal opportunity to share in a virtual room with no limit on how many can gather.

Not that it's perfect. "What even is this place?" mocks one A.A. friend who remains skeptical of the new style. And of course a lot of us miss the historic clubhouse at 1311 York St. where we have so many memories. But for me the question is simple. "Does it work?" And from everything I've seen over these past several months of watching people getting sober in the virtual space and having pretty much the same experience of shared sobriety in a virtual room as we do in the physical space, it has helped me learn to trust in the ability of the virtual space to allow people to get connected and to have a spiritual experience, even for the first time.

Old-timers call it finding your seat. In fact, my sponsor tells me that the most important thing a person can do is to find their seat in the rooms of A.A. and in September, he will have occupied his seat for 40 consecutive years. I've also heard it referred to as occupying a chair. And no doubt one of the reasons why 7am Attitude Adjustment's transition from in-person to online has been so successful is that a lot of the old-timers switched over to the virtual format early in the process and have now found their seat there.

H. for instance - with more than 40 years of continuous sobriety - is now a fixture in the virtual meeting just like he always was in the in-person meeting. And the same is also true for many others who've been occupying their seats at the 7am for at least as long as from when I first arrived in 2007.

Likewise, I also find great benefit in having a home group where I can occupy a chair every day in the same room, although at the in-person 7am I would never get there early enough to sit in the same chair twice! But ever since the stay-at-home orders, it feels like I've shifted from finding my seat in the physical room to finding my seat in the virtual room. Even better, now I'm always able to sit in the same place every morning - a basement room where I'm not disturbing anyone - and over the past four months this has become a sacred space for me equivalent to what the in-person meetings have been all these years. So much so that when Niki happens to come downstairs early to do laundry or whatever, I now tell her that she's profaning a sacred space: Reserved for Recovering Alcoholics Only!

All that's to say that what I've discovered over the past few months is the ability of the virtual spiritual space to stand-in for the physical spiritual space. For the fact is that I can make an exact comparison between my experience going to a meeting every morning in the 7am Attitude Adjustment Zoom room these past few months with my experience of meeting in the 7am Attitude Adjustment at York Street over the past dozen years. And what I have learned is that the virtual space is not deficient, but perhaps equal to, or even in some respects an improvement upon the physical space.

Could it be that this might also be true for the church? For if we also have the potential of having a spiritual experience in a virtual space, might there be similar alternatives for us as well? And considering how much of our time, attention and money we spend maintaining our physical space surely this is something the church needs to consider. Of course meetings of recovery are built on a more sustainable model than is the church - at least in my experience of the established denominational church - primarily because A.A. meetings don't own property, but only rent space.

In fact, its part of the principles of the Twelve Steps and Twelve Traditions, that "An A.A. group ought never endorse, finance or lend the A.A. name to any related facility or outside enterprise, lest problems of money, property and prestige divert us from our primary purpose" (Tradition 6). In my experience, this tradition keeps our A.A. groups from having serious conflict around agendas related to money, or at least not in the same way that I've experienced these conflicts happening at church!

Of course, as a pastor I can't help but to take the message I've heard in the rooms of recovery and apply these same lessons to the church. That being said, I think of what one member of our church's leadership team often asks, which is "What if we opened the church and nobody came?"

Because that's been our experience at the famous York Street clubhouse, where for the past many decades approximately 100 people were there at 7am - rain snow or shine - every morning, 365 days a year. However, now that the club's opened up again, people aren't coming back, and in my experience it's because we already adapted to being in the virtual space. For I can only speak for myself, but if I can have the same spiritual experience virtually as I can in-person, I'm going to choose the more accessible option.

This morning, for instance, we had more than 100 people on our 7am Attitude Adjustment, while at the same time I hear there were less than a dozen people at York Street. Meanwhile online, one young woman spoke up with only 9 days sober. "I know a lot of you don't like online meetings," she said. "But I'm a single mom, who otherwise couldn't be here, and this is saving my ass right now". To me, her share was really powerful, for it reminded me how our primary purpose as a community of faith - whether it's in recovery or in the church - is not just to stay in our comfort zone, but rather to try and be available for the person seeking help.

4

Saturday, March 14, is a day that undoubtedly will always stand out in my memory because this was the day that everything had to pivot from the old style to the new. For even though my friend K. started off that day at 7am by introducing me to Zoom technology, it was totally brand-new to me, so I wasn't comfortable yet using it for broadcasting our Sunday morning service. That's why Niki and I found ourselves spending all day Saturday scrambling to see how best to connect with the congregation online.

It's like the saying "We are NOT all in the same boat" that was a popular meme a few weeks into quarantine. What it means is, while we're all in the same storm we're not all in the same boat, a theme that seemed to apply to just about everything back when everyone was squabbling over our opinions about how soon we should reopen the economy.

For example, the fact we are part of a church family during the pandemic is an example of us all being in the same boat, whereas people who don't have a church family right now are not in the same boat, though they are in the same storm. Likewise, there's a huge difference between those capable of using technology and those who aren't, and unfortunately there's a lot of churches and church people who aren't in the same boat when it comes to technology.

Still, throughout all of our years in ministry, we've come to know many colleagues here and around the country who have far more advanced online operations than what we have here at Central. Many are in large churches with good funding; others have tech-savvy young pastors with mad skills; others have invested in a top-quality technology team and virtual infrastructure. In any case, that's when we started looking to see what our friends were doing online, that Saturday while we were pivoting to decide what's next.

And from what we could tell most of our colleagues also were scrambling just like we were: in fact, it seemed that we were some of the few pastors we knew who were even halfway equipped to consider this question. However, all the other pastors that were part of the conversation shared that they were planning to broadcast out of their sanctuary.

So Niki and I talked, and we seriously considered going to the church and broadcasting from the sanctuary. Then we thought, "Why not just broadcast from our living room and call the program *Worship From Home?*" Because from our perspective, this would be more honest, more authentic, and more true to who we are and what we're going through as well as what everyone else is going through in such a time as this. We deliberated, discerning whether or not we were doing the right thing. Then the next morning we just set up two chairs and an end table in front of our fireplace - it's still cold weather in Denver around the middle of March - lit the fire, turned on my iPhone camera, and let it roll.

Of course it helps that our son, Ezekiel, plays the harp, and as a result we have a beautiful 47-string concert grand harp occupying our living room! Consequently, our son always begins *Worship From Home* by playing on the harp, and this is the first image that grabs people's attention on our video.

No doubt more than anything it was Ezekiel's harp that first brought so much attention to our *Worship From Home* service, at least initially, so it's not something we take for granted. For the fact is Ezekiel is incredibly gifted in many different ways. But most important, our son Ezekiel is one of the sweetest, kindest and most loving human beings we know and we are extremely happy and blessed that he is a member of our family! For while some parents are having a terrible time with their teenagers in quarantine, Ezekiel is really as good-natured and easygoing as a person can be.

At first, we recorded his playing harp from the front so we didn't have to move the camera, but after a few weeks we turned the camera to focus more on his fingers plucking the strings. Again to my mind there's no question that someone playing a concert grand harp to open our worship service and also to play meditative music during the more sacred moments of worship is a huge reason why people tuned in to our broadcast over the past months, thanks be to God.

He has fun with it, too, playing music he learns from video games (Ezekiel is Nintendo's biggest fan) in arrangements suitable for worship. And we pretty much allow him to choose whatever music he wants because we so appreciate his willingness to make a contribution. Ezekiel does play liturgical music, for instance right now he's working on an elaborate arrangement of "The Lord's Prayer," but as just about anything sounds beautiful on the harp we can give him a lot of latitude to choose the music he likes best.

After Ezekiel's prelude, we then turn the iPhone camera to Niki and me. I share a welcome, then Niki has a word of prayer as we open the service of worship. This has been the same format ever since we started, because to my mind it's part of the core message of *Worship From*

Home to present ourselves as a family gathered together in worship.

The theme is evident in the lyrics of an old gospel song we resurrected out of the old-time tradition that has since become a staple of our *Worship From Home* service these last many weeks. Called "The Family Who Prays," the song was first recorded by the Louvin Brothers back in 1958. It shares a message of how "the family who prays will never be parted. Their circle in heaven unbroken shall stand".

Or, in other words, the family that prays together stays together! And this, I believe, is a fundamental part of the message we are sharing through *Worship From Home*. For part of the appeal, I think, is that people are being brought into the home life of a real Christian family where everyone plays a part in praising God, hence we *Worship From Home*. What's more, this is a wonderful opportunity for all of us here in our household to share a sacred time together as a family in a way we've never quite experienced before, and our prayer is that it can be the same for others, as well.

Consequently, we do everything we can to keep it simple, dispensing with any high church ritual that might come across as unnatural. So like everything we do, Niki's prayer to open the service is extemporaneous. Likewise, the songs we sing are performed as a family accompanied by guitar. For the first couple weeks I sang by myself, but as the days went on I invited the family to accompany, which adds a lot especially since Ezekiel has such a strong harmony voice.

We sing three songs together each service, inviting people to join with us in singing. The first song is at the beginning of worship, then one following the message and before communion, then one at the close of the service. From the beginning, and since I didn't have technology that could do things like project words on the screen anyway, I've chosen to sing the most simple old-time gospel songs and hope the people will know these songs, or at least find them familiar.

This means we are singing a lot of country gospel songs that I knew either from back when I was a boy growing up in Georgia, or when I served as a pastor in Tennessee and Kentucky. Songs like "Blessed Assurance"; "Farther Along"; "I'll Fly Away"; or "One Day at a Time" are songs people here and around the world over treasure in our memories, whether we realize it or not. What's more, these songs always seem to work well with a cacophony of voices and because they sound old-fashioned there's a nice synthesis with the janky accompaniment style of an acoustic guitar.

For unlike some of the more sanitized denominational hymns or even most contemporary praise choruses, the old songs carry strong messages of sin and salvation and our hope in the promise of the kingdom of heaven.

That's why I believe people have such deep memories of these old songs because they touched them at some point in their lives that they may not even remember. Plus they are easy to find a harmony! So for all these reasons we sing the old songs.

In fact, soon after I started singing these songs, I heard from both my mom and my dad, who are divorced and live in different states, how much I sound like my Grandaddy Lloyd. For while Lloyd wasn't a preacher, along with my grandmother Carlene he was a popular worship leader at Southern Baptist revivals in the 1950's and 60's. At home he would lead the family in harmonizing to the old hymns, plinking out the accompaniment on his six-string Gibson. "That's the real old-time sound," commented one listener, and I thought, he's right, that's just the way I was taught.

Plus there is really quite a striking contrast between the concert grand harp my son plays in the classical style and the dreadnought acoustic guitar I play in my self-taught country flat-picking style! Forty-seven strings on one and just six on the other. My son Ezekiel, classically trained since he was 5-years-old, versus me as an old-time picker-and-grinner! But it's just an honest reflection of our family.

Likewise, our nine-year-old daughter Eden is very talented. When we first started out she played piano a couple times Sunday morning, however she's now switched from piano to drums. Eden also loves dance, gymnastics, drawing and especially her Golden Retrievers, Sunspot and Soppy. Also I bet Eden spends more time planning her outfit for Sunday mornings than the rest of us put together, for it's important to her that she always finds the right dress for the occasion.

One place Eden regularly participates is by taking part in the Children's Message we have as part of our 10am service each Sunday. At first we didn't think to have a Children's Message, but after a week or two we started inviting Eden to come forward at the start of every program just to have a conversation with her mom about the theme of the day.

Usually Niki has a prop or some other means to engage in conversation on a child's level. She has a lot of skills here because she was a play therapist in her previous career. This is the only part of the service intended specifically for children, and not only does it invite children watching to participate, it gives Eden something she can contribute.

Following the Children's Message, we have a time of sharing local prayer concerns followed by a Pastoral Prayer. This is kind-of a hold-over from our in-person services, and it's something that I still sometimes question as to how well it connects with people online as compared to in-person. However it does provide a time to connect with the needs of the community and to lift people up in prayer, which is an important part of being the church at worship. We share these prayer concerns aloud - first-name-only of course - and then I pray for these concerns and the concerns of the world, closing by leading everyone in the Lord's Prayer.

That's another participatory feature of *Worship From Home:* we ask everyone to say the Lord's Prayer together each Sunday. For as our Lord Jesus said "This is how you should pray" (Matthew 6:9). So as Disciples it's our practice to say the Lord's Prayer each time we gather in worship, as Jesus commanded us to do. Interestingly, Niki and I both say it differently: for where I say the traditional "Our Father" with "forgive us our trespasses"; Niki says "Our Creator" and "forgive us our debts". And of course, one great thing about our church is it's okay - there's no one right way to do it - and I'm glad we represent that diversity of interpretation.

After the prayer, we then read a scripture, and thus far we've mostly been following the readings according to the Revised Common Lectionary, the church-wide calendar of scripture lessons scheduled for the Protestant church day by day. For in my experience, I've found a certain wisdom in following these lessons because it helps guide me away from constantly recycling my own message Sunday after Sunday. Not that I don't read the scriptures through my own lens of interpretation but at least the lectionary gives me a guideline to follow that starts outside my own head.

As a result, I find that people will often ask "How is it that your message was exactly what I needed to hear for this day?" But that's the wisdom of the lectionary, and I trust that there is an underlying intelligence to why these lessons were chosen for these particular times and seasons. What's more, the nature of the lectionary is that it automatically focuses our attention on the major seasons and festivals in the life of the global church - Easter, Pentecost, Christmas, etc. - so that all of us are sharing the same calendar.

While I typically prefer to use the lectionary, in our style of church we reserve the right to share whatever scripture we feel God is calling us to use as we try to catch the wind of the Spirit leading us into this new era of *Worship From Home*. Regardless, I try to keep it simple, limiting the scripture reading to maybe only a few verses at best. And what's more, we will always try to find a lesson and an interpretation that is practical and relevant to the needs of today. For as I often say, "The Bible is not a history book": meaning we wouldn't be reading it if it didn't apply to us!

Next, following the scripture reading - and instead of a traditional sermon - Niki and I will have a conversation about the text going back-and-forth off the top of our heads. We talk together for somewhere around ten minutes having a theological dialogue about the text. It's a very natural conversation, in part because this is something we've been doing for almost twenty-five years since we first met at seminary. For while for the past many years Niki's been a stay-at-home mom and a tireless volunteer at the church, the fact is she's also an ordained minister with a message all her own. People often tell me how much they appreciate Niki's voice, and there's no doubt that having her as a conversation partner is a real strength of our presentation.

Actually I imagine Niki and me having a conversation rather than my just giving a monologue-style sermon is probably something that makes our message a great deal different from many other churches out there. For one thing, sadly there's a lot of places where a woman doesn't have an equal voice to a man or even any voice or opportunity to speak at all. This is true, not only in other parts of the world but also in places here in the U.S. And while no doubt it's something we take for granted in our tradition, when thousands of people are now tuning in to hear our program we have no idea who might become inspired because they see in Niki an example of a woman's voice sharing a message of hope.

Of course, we give thanks that *Worship From Home* provides this opportunity for us, not only because we enjoy our time together, but also because we wouldn't be able to make this kind of impact right now unless we were doing this as a family. For instance, back when were first getting started, I recall our getting a comment on Facebook from someone out-of-state warning us "You need to stay 6-feet apart!" Of course, we wrote back to say we are a married couple and all one family so we can stay as close as we want. Still it was a reminder of just how fortunate we are to have all these different talents working here in the same household: Niki with all her gifts, Ezekiel on the harp and adding his voice, and precious Eden to sing and participate in other ways.

For again, like the song "The Family Who Prays," this image of a family at worship together is itself the message of our service of *Worship From Home*. Because here, in itself, is an image of what a family looks like that prays and worships together. Not that we're perfect, far from it, but in a world that is hurting and desperate for any efforts of good will, just the image of a family at prayer sharing their gifts to worship God makes a strong statement by presenting an encouraging word to people who need a message of hope.

A friend of mine, the pastor of a large church in Florida, tells me how his greatest regret is that, as he puts it, he has never been able to teach the members of his church how to practice their faith at home. He says his people are so dependent on "going to church" that now that they can't put their butts in a pew they just don't know what to do!

In contrast, our family has found a lot of joy out of this time when we've been able to *Worship From Home* together as a family. And while it has its challenges, we are truly blessed that we are able to share this time together, and we pray that our example can be an encouragement to others to be able to worship God with their families together at home.

Sundays after we finish our *Worship From Home*, I often tune in to see what my colleagues are doing out there in the world. And even after four months, what I typically see is a single pastor preaching a manuscript sermon by standing at a lectern and adopting a formal pose. Typically he'll be wearing a suit and preaching a standard sermon, only to an empty room. More elaborate set-ups include musicians and worship leaders accompanying the pastor, either standing apart, social-distanced, or prerecorded at the sanctuary. Other friends with more technological expertise will seam together videos from different sources including readers, musicians, preaching, and testimonials, but for the most part all this is operating out of their church sanctuary.

Worship From Home, however, comes out of a different model. For again, from the very beginning of this pandemic we decided to do this as a deliberate choice in order to be more authentic and more sincere in the way we relate to others in our same situation. So really what we're saying by this style of doing *Worship From Home* is, in fact, "We ARE all in the same boat". For what we find is that when people here and around the the world tune in to Facebook Live to join us in our living room or on our back porch, it somehow communicates the message that we're all in this together.

5

Here we come to the most sacred part of our service of worship: the Lord's Supper. And this, I believe, is a primary ingredient of our church's secret sauce: meaning it's probably one of the main reasons why we are able to offer effective worship online while churches from other more liturgical traditions might be struggling.

That's because the Lord's Supper, or the Eucharist, is something that we as part of the Christian Church (Disciples of Christ) tradition have already come to terms with to such a degree that it wasn't difficult for us to decide what we needed to do in order to share communion. Of course, we believe the Eucharistic meal is the most important part of our worship and for that reason we traditionally hold it as the final ritual of our Sunday morning service. In fact, at the center of our physical sanctuary space in our building on Cherry Creek Drive is a large bronze communion table so large that it resembles a traditional altar, which is typical of Disciples churches.

So, before we ever considered starting an online-only worship service we knew how important it would be to offer communion each time we gather. Actually, I believe that for many Christians access to the Lord's Supper is a large part of why people attend worship, because they're looking for the power that comes with the bread and cup. The question is whether or not it's efficacious, because in order for the Eucharist to transmit real power you have to believe that it is a true representation of the Body of Christ.

Roman Catholics, for instance, are very particular about the efficacy of the Lord's Supper. Catholics mandate that the sacred host must be received from a sanctioned priest at an officially church-sanctioned Mass in order to be efficacious. A Catholic friend once told me how he so wished the priest would offer the sacred host in the first five minutes of Mass so that he and his family could just keep their coats on, take communion, and split! His comment reminded me that for many people the main reason they come to church is for the Lord's Supper. However when the churches are closed, for those that restrict the efficacy of communion to only that which is specially meted out by a certified priest, it thus becomes impossible to partake of the Lord's Supper.

That's why we see Roman Catholics during this time of social-distancing having to issue a dispensation allowing people to be free from the requirement to take communion from a Catholic priest. When I heard that, I said to my wife: "Of course, we Protestants have had that freedom now for 500 years". Turns out it was only expediency, not efficacy, that finally allowed the Roman Catholic hierarchy to relax their restrictions on how people can take communion.

In much the same way, I believe we are all of us now going through a new reformation in the larger church in which we are finally being freed of our idolatry of the church as a building. The first reformation, 500 years ago, freed the church from the tyranny of priests and bishops. Since then, Protestant movements such as the stream that we're part of in the Disciples of Christ have continued to free the church from clericalism, in that we have allowed the table of the Eucharist to become the people's table, where no priests are required to preside. Yet there is still much to be done.

For while the first reformation was intended to correct abuses of ecclesiastic authority under the Roman Catholic church, in transferring the authority of the church from the priests to the laity they did not yet recognize the potential of just regular folks to abuse our authority. However, over the past 500 years or so we've learned how congregational autonomy is far from the utopian model the Reformers had envisioned. For in my experience with both Congregational and Baptist traditions, I've seen how easily well-meaning laypeople and volunteers will acquiesce to the rule of the bully - even the rule of the mob - aka *The Lord of the Flies*.

Sadly, this is the experience of all too many pastors in the congregational church system of being chewed up and spit out by the bullies who own the church. How often have we heard, "Remember who pays your salary!" Or how often have we heard a story about the Baptist Board of Deacons calling a meeting in the middle of the night to fire their poor pastor because they didn't like his Sunday sermon.

For imperfect as pastors might be, stories like these remind us that pastoral leadership is God-ordained for the church. Not only is this how the church was established in the New Testament (see Hebrews 13:11; also 1 Timothy 5:17-18), in my experience laypeople often need a pastor to help moderate disputes in a congregation as well as to help keep people focused on the prerogatives of the Word of God rather than their own opinions and perspectives. For while pastors are human too, at least it's our job to try and remain objective.

In contrast, the apparent mobocracy some churches call their Board of Deacons is typically something far short of the New Testament ideal for the church. In fact, it may be that every human attempt to enshrine God in a structure propped up with a system of rules and regulations and call it church is something short of what God is calling us to be (consider the Tower of Babel story in Genesis 11; or Peter's desire to build structures to contain God's glory in Luke 9).

Recognizing this, the movement that became our church - the Christian Church (Disciples of Christ) - was birthed out of late 18th-century Scots-Presbyterian reformers desire to return to the simple faith of the first-century church. Fed up with the hierarchy of the Presbyterian establishment, our ancestors vowed to get back to the Bible by rejecting all human authority in qualifying pastors for leadership.

History recalls that this freedom regarding the Lord's Table is why our church movement spread across the United States so quickly in the Frontier era, because we gave folks the opportunity to take communion without access to priests. This is in adherence to our understanding of what it means to be "the priesthood of all believers"(1 Peter 2:9). And while over the past 200 years, the Disciples of Christ have again created a hierarchical leadership structure, we are alone among the Protestants in having dispensed with all hierarchy of status in the celebration of the Lord's Table.

Believe it or not but still now, more than 200 years after our movement's founding in 1803, our interpretation of the Lord's Table that allows "whoever will" to commune with God continues to be too radical for most other

Protestants and remains something entirely unique to our church's expression in the larger Protestant communion. For example, my mother, an Episcopal priest, was required to serve a whole year ordained a deacon (an obligatory commitment following graduation from seminary) before she was allowed to be ordained as a priest. Only then did she become authorized to preside over the sacred host.

In contrast, in the Christian Church (Disciples of Christ) not only do we put no restrictions around who can commune at the table, we technically have no restrictions over who can preside at the table. For as far as I know, our movement is still the only one that welcomes laypeople to preside at the communion table without status. In this we recognize that this is not our table but Christ's table and Christ's invitation, for "God is no respecter of persons" (Acts 10:34).

Again, this freedom that we celebrate at the Lord's Table is something that would seem too radical in many churches even to this day. For you can tell by these examples how we in the Christian Church (Disciples of Christ) exercise a lot more liberty here than do Christians of other movements.

For example, years ago I was interviewing for a church position with a recruiter who came out of the Lutheran church. And after some conversation, learning I was a Disciple, he asked, "So how then, with the practice of open communion, do you practice discipline in the church?"

He was a Lutheran and, as he explained, in their tradition communion is "the primary mechanism of discipline" determining who's in and who's out. Consequently, he did not understand how we as Disciples could possibly maintain discipline and order in our fellowship without proscribing who could partake at the table.

In response, I shared with him the story of one of the founders of our church tradition, Alexander Campbell, who surrendered his Presbyterian clergy credentials because he was unwilling to deny hospitality to anyone seeking the Lord's Supper. "The Story of the Tossed Communion Token" took place almost 220 years ago and is a foundational story of our movement representing a rejection of any human jurisdiction over the Lord's Supper.

For as Disciples of Christ, we recognize that the sacred communion meal is not something that can be set apart and guarded by authorities. Again, as we say each time we gather, "It is Christ's table, not our table" and consequently it is by Christ's invitation we are invited. Of course, Christ's invitation is something discerned within each individual heart, not something any human determination can decide.

To that end, in Disciples churches even children have been seen presiding at the Lord's Table. Our Biblical mandate for this practice, unique in the larger church, is that our Lord said "Let the little children come to me" (Matthew 10:34), for we believe that God's grace is mediated by Christ alone.

All that's to say that we as Disciples seem to approach the communion table differently than many other Christians. Meaning that, whereas other traditions may have rules and restrictions that keep them from having the liberty to take communion virtually, as Disciples we believe we are free from any constraints as to how we practice communion.

For instance, at the start of every Sunday service we invite everyone to bring their own elements for communion and then we welcome them to partake of those elements - whatever they may be - simultaneously together with us in our worship broadcast. Particularly when we first started *Worship From Home* we made a big deal of reaching out to invite members and friends to share what they were taking for communion, whether it was cereal and milk, juice and cookies, or wine and crackers. We ourselves also use various elements - like pop tarts and all manner of items, whatever we have around - as an effort to model the freedom we have in Christ to partake of the bread and cup.

Still, more than anything, inviting people to share what elements they were taking for communion was our way to allow them to be active participants in *Worship From Home*. For because we are not joining together in person, we want to do everything we possibly can to help people to feel a part of the community. Asking people to share the elements together online is thus perhaps the primary way that we are able to invite them to participate in a virtual setting, and we hope that it helps people feel like they are able to be active in worship, even while we are teaching by example that God doesn't need a consecrated host to impart grace.

It worked, in that after that first service we got a lot of feedback that people felt like they were being invited when we asked them to share their communion elements with us online. Maybe this is really the true magic of holding these services in the online room and inviting people to partake with whatever they have on hand. For by asking people to provide their own elements for bread and cup, you are actually inviting them to become active participants in the sacred rite of the Lord's Supper, the Eucharist.

So it is that, by inviting people to find the communion elements in common goods from their own home we are thereby imparting a revolutionary theological point, albeit subliminally, that the invitation to the Lord's Supper comes from Christ himself and therefore is not something anyone owns. We also make this distinction at the physical Lord's Table each time we gather in the sanctuary, for I believe it's important to remind people that we come, not at our invitation but at Christ's invitation. Because this table does not belong to us but to God, through Jesus Christ Himself.

Again, Roman Catholics require a particular dispensation if congregants are to go without partaking of the sacred host distributed from the hand of the priest and yet remain faithful. Likewise, others in traditions that require the mediation of a priest to sanctify the host may not feel they have the option to take communion virtually. That's why some churches go to such elaborate lengths to provide prepackaged consecrated elements to the congregants.

In contrast, because Disciples dare to set aside the role of priests in consecrating the communion bread and cup we are often misunderstood by the more liturgical traditions. For example, my mom tells us that when she shared with a group of Episcopal priest friends about our church inviting people to provide their own elements, they responded with dismay. "Does that mean they could use milk and cookies?" one of them replied with a sneer. "The sacrilege!"

For whether or not we appreciate it, people in our tradition seem to welcome the opportunity to take communion at home, and what's more we have no problem using diverse elements to represent the bread and cup.

And while no doubt we take it for granted, fortunately our church tradition seems to have already digested some of the theological and existential questions that are necessary for the church to transcend the idea that communion is only efficacious when it is distributed in a particular form.

That being said, whenever we share communion during *Worship From Home* we always do it at the close of the service in the same way we normally would do it in-person worship. Typically, Niki gives a brief meditation - something that was in her thoughts that week or a recent experience - to connect the act of communion with our day-to-day life. After her meditation, then I share the Words of Institution, traditional words spoken in memory of Jesus at the Lord's Supper (from 1 Corinthians 11:23-26) while Ezekiel plays instrumental music on his harp in the background.

Following the Words of Institution, I break the bread and share the cup - looking into the camera all the while - then I will share the bread and the cup with Niki, saying "The body of Christ, broken for you. The blood of Christ, shed for you". Niki then shares the bread and the cup with me, though she uses different words, saying something like, "The bread of life and the cup of peace". Again, this is an indication of the diversity of perspective that we represent between ourselves as a couple, which is in itself a witness to our welcome of theological diversity. Next we share the elements with

Eden, and then I turn and symbolically share the bread and cup with all those who are watching online.

All the while, Ezekiel is accompanying this ritual with soft meditative music on his harp. Following communion, we close the service with another song that we sing as a family while I accompany on guitar. This allows Eden to join us again at the close of the service which always adds a lot of energy to our presentation. Often I'll choose a simple, up-tempo chorus for the closing song - it helps if its something that Eden already knows how to sing - and at times I'll even ask the kids to play rhythm instruments. My hope is that our closing song will lift people up and encourage them, providing a contrast to the somber note of communion.

Finally, after the closing song, I share the benediction and Ezekiel finishes with another piece on the harp. The whole service lasts about forty-five minutes. Typically only a tiny percentage of those who ultimately watch the service are watching it live, but we enjoy getting comments and likes from those participants in real time. Meanwhile, others will join in later in their own time or even in another time zone.

6

In any case, all that is to say how our *Worship From Home* service is something that came about entirely organically as an offshoot of the traditional prerogatives of our church, as well as the talents we felt we had available to us when we first found ourselves stranded at home with nothing but our musical instruments and our cellphones.

That's why, for the first several weeks after we started *Worship From Home* we did the 10 o'clock service just as we described - sitting in front of the fire in the living room - because I felt the fireplace was our most homey setting for a March morning in Colorado. Also, and as I mentioned, I believe our son Ezekiel's harp played a huge part in why our church first attracted attention, for not many people under quarantine have a 47-string concert grand harp in their living room and someone who knows how to play it!

From what we hear, a lot of what is attractive to people is that we're doing this from our living room, and that we're not trying to be anything or anyone we're not. And in much the same way, when we first started stay-at-home orders, I took the opportunity to go natural with my appearance, in contrast to dressing up for church. My rationale was that with everyone just sitting at home in their pajamas it would be unnatural for us to dress up because the whole premise of *Worship From Home* is to meet people where they are. So with that in mind, instead of my typical clean-shaven face, button-down shirt, and khakis, I would wear a denim shirt, jeans, and also went without shaving for about 3 weeks.

Things seemed to be going pretty well - we were getting 600-700 views of our worship each week, far more than we would have in-person - so I continued not to shave, figuring it signified how we're all in the same boat. That is until after about 3 Sundays when I got a call from Bob Dumler. And he said, "Son" - he always calls me son - he said "don't forget all this church business is just a sales game! You need to clean up your act - shave your face and put on a clean white shirt - and you'll get a lot more people tuning in. Because nobody wants to see you up there looking like a bum!"

At first I was annoyed at Bob for reprimanding me. Thank God he didn't tell me to cut my hair, otherwise I probably would have told him where he could put it! But Bob's an old hippie - he doesn't mind my long hair -

he only wanted me to present myself better. Later I found out it was actually Peggy's idea that I clean up my appearance, she just didn't want to be the one to say something to me and thought I'd take the suggestion better coming from Bob.

Regardless, I took their suggestion and the next week, which was the last service Peggy saw before she died, I showed up clean shaven and wearing a clean white shirt, the same as I always did in in-person worship. For the fact is that's the way I was brought up and the way I was trained in ministry I would never have thought of leading worship or even going to church if I wasn't clean and pressed! So I guess in some ways God ordained that this priority needed to continue under *Worship From Home*, represented by me continuing to shave my face and to wear a clean white shirt.

And our viewership responded. For instance the Sunday I finally cleaned up my act, Palm Sunday, we got 2200 viewers of our Facebook Live service, which was triple the amount we had the Sunday before. This was not as a direct result of my making this change, but I took it as a sign from God that we were doing the right thing and that we have been listening for God's voice in prompting us with the best answers in order to maximize the potential for spreading the message in these times. And from my experience there seem to be a lot of indications like this, or ways where it seems like God is prompting us in the way we should go.

But before we go any further, I should probably tell the story of how Peggy passed, because there's no doubt in my mind that without Peggy we wouldn't be where we are today. For as I've shared, this book is written in memory of Peggy, for as the church Moderator she walked with me through the excruciating fires of the past two years. In fact, Peggy took as much criticism if not more than I did simply for serving in her volunteer role of protecting the interests of the church. Then, not even a month into the coronavirus pandemic stay at home orders, on the Monday following Palm Sunday, Peggy passed over into her eternal reward.

For as I mentioned, even after all the hard work Peggy had done and had driven us to do, when we asked why she was still working so hard, she would always say that she was taking care of the defense so that Cameo, whom she was mentoring to be our next Moderator, would be able to use her gifts to play offense. To that end, we tied up the loose ends in every possible area, taking care of facility needs, security, vulnerabilities in the bylaws, and using everything we learned to protect the church. And in order to do this, Peggy gave countless hours. In fact, I would not be at all surprised if she was working for the church as many as 40 hours and probably no less than 20 hours on most weeks.

Which brings us to the conversation Peggy and I had on April 4th, the Saturday before Palm Sunday. (Ironically it was Palm Sunday 2 years before, in 2018, that all hell broke loose in the church). And since Holy Week is the most sacred time of the Christian year, and our busiest time as well, we took the opportunity to talk for almost two hours.

This was not unusual for us, in fact I joked that Peggy and I could never get off the phone in less than 45 minutes, but I remember this conversation as special because it ranged over such a wide range of topics. That Saturday we talked about everything from the footwashing service we did on Maundy Thursday two years ago - where Peggy and I knelt down to wash the feet of the people who had betrayed us - to the fact it was now two years since all these hardships happened and all that has been accomplished since then.

We talked about her 97 year old father, Herb, and how he was doing in the nursing home; about the concerns they had around their business under the stay-at-home orders; and she mentioned how great she felt with the progress she was making exercising in her home gym. At that point we had only done *Worship From Home* a couple of weeks, but we talked about how after all the trials we had faced over the past couple years we really didn't have any fear about what comes next. Because when you've been through as hard of things as we've been through together, then you know you'll be able to adjust to whatever life might bring.

Already Peggy was amazed at the response we had seen in just a couple weeks broadcasting our service on Facebook at 10am. She found it to be really exciting that we were already seeing 600 and 700 views of our worship service every week. "This is the future of our church!" she said. "Can you believe we already have the infrastructure in place to take us where God is leading us?" she continued.

She was so proud that we had had no delay in the transition to *Worship From Home*. "There's no doubt in my mind that God is inviting us to share our message with all the world. I'm so excited to see what's coming". For somehow Peggy could see it even before I saw that these circumstances of COVID-19 pandemic were guiding us into our future story.

Again this was the Saturday before Palm Sunday when we'd yet to have more than 700 views of a worship service. So I remember how excited I was that Sunday night to tell Peggy about the numbers. "Peggy's right," I recall saying to Niki that evening, because after seeing that increase in viewers just that one Sunday I realized the potential for growth.

The next day was Monday, which is normally my day off, but as I mentioned I go to my A.A. meeting every morning at 7 AM, so I had just gotten off the A.A. meeting to sit at my desk in the downstairs office when at about 8:15am my cell phone rings and it says "Bob Dumler". Strange, I thought, because Bob never calls, however as I would often talk with Peggy first thing in the morning I just assumed it was Peggy calling me on Bob's phone as she would sometimes do.

So I answered the phone, and there was Bob on the line and he said "Peggy's dead," and I said something like, "Sure we're all of us feeling wiped out, aren't we?" or something like that. Then he says, "No, she's laying here next to me, dead". And I say something like, "Well, I'm sure she's probably so tired she feels like she's dead". So then Bob raises his voice and says, "Damn it, son! I'm telling you that Peggy's laying right here next to me, and she's dead!"

Unfortunately it wasn't until that point that I finally got it. "I'm so sorry," I said. "I can't believe it". He told me it happened on her exercise equipment that morning. At that point she had passed less than a half hour before and the paramedics were still finishing up. Again, just Saturday she told me how she felt she was in the best shape of her life working out from home. She was 67 years old with no pre-existing conditions. And she was probably my best friend in the world, besides my wife Niki. We talked everyday - we'd been through the fire together - and she saw the promise of this future although she was not able to enter into it herself.

That was Monday of Holy Week, which meant that Peggy's passing happened on the same week as Maundy

Thursday, Good Friday, and everything else that built up to Easter Sunday. What's more, we also had to do all these worship services and events virtually for the first time ever. Already I had promised to lead the men in a virtual version of our traditional Living Last Supper drama where we have 12 men play the role of the disciples, and I knew I had to figure this out on Zoom technology that was altogether new to me.

Later that same day, I went over to Bob's house to have a social-distanced visit on his back porch. This was the first in-person visit that I had made to a parishioner since the quarantine and since Bob was in the vulnerable category of a man over age 70, I did everything I knew how at the time to keep an appropriate distance. Meaning we had our visit on the back deck, stayed 6 feet apart, and I wore a bandana over my mouth, the only face-covering I had at the time.

What struck me most about the visit was how their house and their neighborhood was just the same as it ever was, as if nobody knew that Peggy had died. And while I've often had this impression visiting after a death, this time it was stronger than usual, probably because I hadn't been out of the house much in the three weeks prior to visiting Bob.

Of course, there wasn't really anything to say - there never is in these types of circumstances - however as there was no option to have an in-person memorial service under that stage of the stay-at-home orders in Colorado, we decided it was best to do Peggy's memorial service on Zoom, and scheduled it for Friday morning starting at 10am so it could be finished in time for our Good Friday service at noon.

Peggy's Zoom memorial service was now my number one priority for Holy Week. But since I'd never done anything like this before, and had already committed to reviving the Living Last Supper drama on this new technology, I spent the next three days focusing most of my attention on figuring out how to use Zoom. In fact, Thursday night it really felt like I was cramming down to the wire as I struggled to edit the Zoom video to post it online while getting ready for the two worship services the next day.

Yet despite the tight schedule, the truth is it was very meaningful to be able to prepare the memorial service as well as to work on the technology required to pre-record the Living Last Supper drama which simultaneously gave me the experience and confidence I needed to run the memorial service the following day. For this was a very personal loss for me as well, and sometimes what's best for us in a season of grief is to stay focused on the task at hand.

That week I also reached out to talk with my mom on the phone, something I don't know that I'd done since the pandemic first started. Mom is a retired Episcopal priest and our conversation often touches on theological matters. What's more, although I don't talk with her that regularly, I often will reach out to her in seasons of particular stress.

So I shared with her what happened, and as we were talking I saw the image in my mind of Peggy looking down from the mountaintop over into the Promised Land. For just like Moses, she could see the future but just wasn't able to get there (Deuteronomy 32:49). At that point, I recalled Peggy's and my conversation Saturday when she was so excited about the future. For Peggy had caught a vision of the future, and that Saturday morning Peggy could see that vision clearly and was excited about what we had in store.

"Oh yes, it's very appropriate to remember Peggy as your Moses!" Mom said. "Because as the leader of your church, it was Peggy that brought you out of slavery in the Land of Egypt!" For Mom knows how Peggy fought the good fight against the church bullies, standing in the fire to help us get where we needed to go. What's more, Peggy was God's instrument to free the church from bondage to those legacy dynamics that ruled our decision-making for so long. So Mom's right - that's another way Peggy was our Moses - for somebody had to say: "Let my people go" (Exodus 8:1)!

In any case, it was an apt analogy, so at the service Friday I shared the scripture about how "Moses was a man after Gods own heart" (Acts 13:22) and asked that we remember Peggy as the Moses of our church these past many years. Cameo had prerecorded a slideshow with photo memories of Peggy, and we had Ezekiel prerecord a piece on the harp, plus I got some song lyrics together to share on my screen.

Beforehand, I was worried that the technology would be a problem because we were hearing so much about "Zoom-bombing" in those early weeks of quarantine. Also, since we had experienced so much conflict in the church, I was wary of what we might hear from certain antagonists in the wake of Peggy's passing. So I was more than a little anxious as we prepared for our first ever Zoom memorial service.

That being said, the fact is it turned out to be one of the most meaningful and personal memorial services we've ever had. We started with Ezekiel's prerecorded solo at 10am, then transitioned to Cameo's beautiful photo memorial. Next we opened it up for sharing our memories, I gave a simple eulogy, and we closed with a song.

In the end, around 50 different Zoom screens joined us for about an hour-and-a-half of sharing, and the fact is it was actually far more intimate than it would have been at an in-person service, which may be the silver-lining of this style of memorial. Several people suggested that God must have needed someone like Peggy to organize hospitality up there in heaven because of all the people dying from COVID-19. Likewise, I like to image her up there pulling levers for us to open up the floodgates of God's blessings for our church!

Afterwards, we posted the video slideshow Cameo made up on our church Facebook page and we also put the memorial service video up on a private Facebook page so that Peggy's friends could watch it over again. We are also requesting donations to refurbish our church's historic bell-tower as a memorial in Peggy's honor, with a ceremony we plan to hold towards the end of summer. Furthermore, this book is dedicated to Peggy and is written in her memory.

Still, as hard as all of this was, it was at this point that I first began to see some of the silver linings in regards to having virtual rather than in-person services. For having not only Peggy's memorial, but also the Living Last Supper drama Maundy Thursday and then Good Friday all together back to back over Holy Week was a very poignant experience.

Looking back, I can see how having Peggy's memorial service on Zoom so early into our experience of *Worship From Home* helped confirm to me that just because a service or meeting is in the virtual rather than in the physical space doesn't make it any less meaningful. And amazingly, this is yet another way Peggy helped to guide us into God's future. For even in her death, she gave us an example of how to faithfully roll with the changes.

7

Perhaps it's presumptuous of me to say, but it feels like God has been looking out for us all along. For example, when we first started *Worship From Home*, we didn't have any equipment other than my old refurbished iPhone 6 to record the service. Worse than the video quality, however, was the audio on the first few broadcasts mainly because we didn't have an external microphone.

Of course, we didn't have a regular tripod either, instead we attached the iPhone to an old selfie-stick we duct-taped to a microphone stand. The audio quality was so poor, however, that the second week we tried to fix it by rigging up a regular microphone to a loudspeaker. We then built a tower of books stacked on top of a stool to raise the speaker to the height of the iPhone and then pointed the speaker directly at the iPhone in an effort to improve the sound!

We would have found better equipment, but unfortunately at that time we were limited in where we could shop for supplies. Stores deemed non-essential were closed, and Amazon had delayed all of their normal shipping times to prioritize COVID-19 related supplies. So it took about three weeks before we were able to acquire a simple ten dollar external microphone to plug-in to the iPhone. Just that little change, however, made our sound quality so much better.

At the same time, we bought a tripod with an attachment for an iPhone as well as a large light ring, all of which arrived around the same time as the microphone. Of course the peripherals made an improvement in our presentation; however for the first 6 weeks or so of *Worship From Home* we still used that same old iPhone 6 for all of our recording.

That is until I dropped it one morning, right as the service was starting, and it literally broke in half right down the seam, and also cracked the screen. Somehow I managed to snap it back together and amazingly it worked to record the service. However, I was obviously rather annoyed, or at least anyone who knew me would have been able to tell that I was frustrated about something on the video. Again, this was a little later in the cycle - probably about 6 weeks in - but what happened as a result of my breaking my iPhone was really incredible, and I'm glad to tell the story.

Probably the reason I dropped the phone that day was because I was anxious. Over the past few weeks we had started getting a greater number of views on Facebook - I think it was 7500 or so just the Sunday before - and so as I was setting up the iPhone in the tripod I was excited to think about how so many people were watching. Yet because this was something so new, I got overexcited, and my hand shook and dropped the phone. And while I was able to put the phone back together in time to make the recording, I had a bad attitude about it.

In any case, I remember catching myself on camera during that service actually scowling at the screen because I was so annoyed I had broken my phone. In fact, I was so disappointed with myself that I said to Niki afterwards, "Let's just scrap this recording and do it over again".

Yet afterwards we watched as we got more views on that video than we've ever had before, something like 10,000. Later people told me it was their favorite service because I was obviously so annoyed that it made it seem more real. In the end it was a huge lesson for me that I'm not in control.

Even more interesting was that as soon as I hung up the phone and as we finished recording the live video I got a call from a man saying, "Let me buy you a new phone!" Then, while he was talking, I was interrupted from another call and when I took that call and it was someone else saying "Let me buy you a new phone!" And because the second person was somebody new to the church I let them have the opportunity. Amazingly, later that same afternoon I got another call from yet another person asking if I would please let them buy me a phone!

That being said, the reason this story needs to be told is as an example of how people's generosity continues to support the church. Plus it shows how God is providing for the needs of this ministry in real-time and helping us as we reach out to the larger group. For that's the whole point, that through this project God is teaching us a lesson that our strength is not in ourselves, but that God is making a way for us somehow, sometimes even despite ourselves.

Amazingly, how God works is that even those things we might perceive as a set-back, such as breaking my iPhone, end up being a way to further God's plan and purpose. In this case, my complaining about the phone on Facebook Live resulted in someone buying the new technology that's actually made a real difference in our sharing the message.

Niki says she worries this might encourage me to complain more loudly in hopes of receiving a reward! But I don't think so: instead, to me it was just evidence that God is using even our brokenness to further the Divine purpose. In fact, it's the kind of thing I'll probably always remember because it was a lesson in what we call

"Rule 62" (which is A.A. shorthand for "Don't Take Yourself So Seriously!").

"Rule 62" is yet another A.A. aphorism meant to point us in the direction of truth. And while outsiders may find these to be silly, sayings like this or "Think, Think, Think" (which a friend of mine in long-term sobriety interprets to mean "three thinks and you're out") are all access points to finding a different way of thinking through 12-step recovery.

For while there is no particular connection between the program of recovery and *Worship From Home*, to me they are the same in that both are about connecting to the same power. For in my experience, the same power that keeps me sober is the same power that led our church through the storms of the past two years, and that same power is opening the doors to the revival we are experiencing today.

Recovering alcoholics know about power, for the reason we are alcoholic is because we lost the power to drink. *The Big Book* says "Lack of power, that was our dilemma" (pg. 45). Consequently, alcoholics seek after God in order to find the strength to overcome our drinking problem. Since real alcoholism means a person no longer has any control over taking the first drink, the alcoholic must sincerely seek God or else he will drink, and for an alcoholic to drink is to die.

It works when you work it, that's my experience, and it does the same for others as well, otherwise why would 100 people climb 3 flights of stairs every day at 7am just to go to a meeting? For as I said, the 7am Attitude Adjustment I helped K. get started on Saturday, March 14 grew quickly under stay-at-home orders to as many as 160 people every morning at 7am. This is not the largest Zoom meeting of A.A., not by far. In fact, I've heard of A.A. meetings on Zoom as large as 1700 people and there are many of 1000 people or more. But this is my home group, the same meeting I've attended at 7am almost every day for 10 years.

In other words, for the past 10 years I've been getting up early every morning, at times to shovel the driveway and clean the snow off my car, then driving 25 minutes in rush-hour traffic before circling around the neighborhood a few times to find off-street parking in Capitol Hill. Then I would walk several blocks in all kinds of weather to the clubhouse before walking up three flights of stairs to then squeeze into one of the 120 or so folding chairs that were crammed into every nook and cranny of the crowded second-story room.

York Street is a particularly famous A.A. clubhouse where I've seen a few celebrities walk through the doors and I've seen a lot of hard luck cases come and go as well. And like anything, there's really no substitute for actually being there in-person. That's why I detailed the effort I would make - day in and day out - to get there each day under normal circumstances, as did everyone else that was there. Because there's something I gained by this experience, namely my sobriety, that kept me coming back.

What I'm saying is there is real power in A.A. which is why people like me keep coming back day after day year after year. "The central fact of our lives today is the absolute certainty that our Creator has entered into our hearts and minds in a way which is indeed miraculous," writes Bill W. (*The Big Book*, pg. 25). For "the spiritual life is not a theory. We have to live it" (pg. 83). And once we finally get it, by the grace of God, we discover a relationship in which "God is doing for us what we cannot do for ourselves" (pg. 84).

Practically speaking, what this means is that I can cultivate a relationship with a power greater than myself that will fight my battles for me. In fact, it says in *The Big Book* that "we have stopped fighting anyone or anything" (pg. 103). Consequently, we can now "relax and take it easy" (pg. 86) because we trust that God will handle our business for us.

All this allows me to find the hope and faith that, so long as I can just show up and do my part, everything is going to work out. The 12-step model thus provides a very practical and contemporary take on spirituality that, above all else, reminds us not to carry burdens too heavy for us to bear. For if nothing else, you will find in

A.A. people who will empathize with your plight, knowing that a burden shared is a burden halved, yet without cosigning on your misery.

Perhaps this explains why the rooms of A.A. have been my primary touchstone as to the importance of keeping a room open and available for those who are still suffering. Not that I'm an expert, by any means. In fact, part of the way that A.A. works is that there are no experts. "This is not a guru program," we like to say, which is a lot of the reason why it can be so helpful to people like doctors or priests or other professionals, because we don't have to play the expert. I have, however, had a front row seat for the transition from in-person to online in both the church and the rooms of recovery, almost as if I was given a particular vantage point.

So it was that, at first, I watched more closely to determine the potential success of online A.A. meetings in helping people to maintain sobriety than I was concerned about the success of our online church. That's because I see sobriety as the spiritual foundation of my work and responsibility in ministry. As a result, when we first started online meetings I had all kinds of anxiety because I still wasn't confident as to whether these online meetings could really work.

However, it wasn't until I saw people joining the meetings, people I've seen coming in and out the doors of York Street for years now, and heard some of them sharing honestly - perhaps for the first time - that I started to believe these meetings could work as well on Zoom as in-person. One guy in particular I've seen come and go from the rooms dozens of times over the past ten years though he's always hung his head down low so I've never heard him speak. So I was surprised to see how much easier it seems for him now on Zoom. Because now that we're online he shows up every day with a smile on his face, joining in the fun, and most importantly he has over 30 days continuous sobriety!

Even better is when someone joins our Zoom meeting with no prior experience of in-person A.A. meetings and gets sober in the virtual room. Again, for me, that's the key question, as the whole reason I'd get up every morning and go through the process I described to get to a meeting is because it works! So if people can get sober by going to a virtual meeting just as well as by going to an in-person meeting, then that's all I really need to know, because the whole point of the meeting is so people can get sober.

In other words, all that really matters is that it works, so as long as it works it doesn't make any difference where you have it. Yet how convenient it is at 7am just to join in your pajamas, or on your morning walk, or having breakfast, or driving to work or whatever you might be doing, in contrast to all of the driving, parking, walking, climbing stairs and jockeying for a seat that was required just to get into the rooms in the days before coronavirus social-distancing.

I remember many times getting to York Street after all of that journey only to find that there were no seats, so I had to stand outside the room or sit on the stairs. And while it's definitely a good problem to have when people are beating down the doors to get sobriety at 7am, it just goes to show how there's always limited space in the physical room compared to how many can join in the virtual room online.

These days, too, we'll often hear people share about how it used to be they could only join with us once a week, or how they had moved away and haven't found a comparable fellowship in their new area, but with the online meetings geography and other considerations are now no longer a barrier to their participation. Truckers now join us from the road and people tune in from their hospital beds. Already we can see a lot of positives to having the meetings online, especially when it comes to questions of equal access.

In much the same way, we're finding that people can more easily connect to church online through *Worship From Home* either simultaneous with the broadcast or on their own schedule later in the day or anytime they choose. Likewise, people can share communion with us in real time using their own elements, but they can also participate on their own time and even chime in to the worship service after the fact with a comment on the video and we will get back with them. Actually, we've heard from many people of how they feel more intimacy, more personal connection being invited into our living room warts-and-all than they did when we were putting on our best Brady Bunch smile and wearing our Sunday-school-clothes in the sanctuary.

So we give God all the glory! For just like in the online A.A. meetings, the question is whether or not the new format of *Worship From Home* even works, and from the response we've had so far it seems it does. Because clearly, it's not about us, there's a lot of evidence to confirm that. For as I mentioned, that one Sunday I dropped my phone and had a scowl on my face we had more views than we ever have before - significantly more - reminding us that what we are doing is not so much about excellence in presentation as it is about authenticity and being ourselves. In fact, my guess is more people tuned in that day because of the comedic value of the episode than did for probably anything else!

And God continues to provide. For as the scripture says, "Seek first the kingdom of God and His righteousness and all these things will be added to you" (Matthew 6:33). So whenever we receive unexpected financial blessings I tend to take it as a sign we are on the right path. That's why, as I mentioned, when 3 different people offered to buy me a phone that day, in the end I decided to take up the offer of someone new to the church who really pressed the issue, saying they wanted to "receive the blessing" they believe comes with supporting the work of the ministry financially.

This is a big deal, because a new phone is not the type of thing a pastor can readily ask the church to provide, although in these circumstances it's become an absolutely necessary tool of ministry. Private donors, however, can respond far more quickly to an immediate need like an advance in technology, which is something that typically goes by the wayside in a church's decisions around budget.

This same couple, who choose to remain anonymous, also bless many others in the life of the church with direct gifts and financial help as they find their joy in being generous. Tangible helps like these from person to person have represented a special affirmation in this time of pandemic, when many people are struggling from loss of income.

Furthermore, although we're no longer able to pass the plates on Sunday morning, I've been pleased to watch as our members have continued to contribute to our budget by mail and are learning how to make donations online. At first, the church saw a slow-down in contributions as we were all just waiting to see what would happen next. But now that we're adjusting to a new normal our contributions are back up to normal levels and increasing all the time.

Even better, we are starting to get unsolicited donations from places near and far. For instance, over the weekend we got a request totally out-of-the blue for a pledge card from a person who was previously connected with our church but had been out of touch for years. That is until the quarantine when she found us again online. So to me, this was a sign that we will have everything we need so long as we continue to trust in God's providence (see Malachi 3:10).

8

From all these things we've seen happening the past couple months to promote *Worship From Home*, it sure seems like somebody's been pulling some levers for us up there! For somehow, seemingly miraculously, ever since Peggy passed away we've watched our message extend to a larger and larger audience here and around the world.

That Sunday after Peggy passed was Easter, and as I mentioned earlier we had already announced our schedule for Holy Week which was to include a virtual Easter Sunrise Service, as that was a tradition we had established rather successfully the year before. What's more, because we were doing *Worship From Home* this year I checked to see when the actual sunrise was that day because I thought here's an opportunity to do our Sunrise Service actually at sunrise, which that day was scheduled for around 6:28 AM.

Consequently we scheduled our Easter Sunrise Service for 6:30am with the plan that it would be about fifteen minutes long with a couple songs on guitar, prayer, scripture and a brief message. And because my son Ezekiel has such a good harmony vocal I conscripted him to roll out of bed a little early that morning and help me with the presentation.

If I recall, between the Sunrise Service at 6:30am and our regular 10am *Worship From Home* service that day we gained a total of 7500 views of these videos on Facebook: 4500 for the 10am service and 3000 for the Sunrise Service. That was up from 2200 of the *Worship From Home* service the Sunday before, up from 700 views of that same service the Sunday before. What's more, I noticed that a larger percentage of those who watch the Sunrise Service watched it all the way through or for a longer length of time perhaps in part because it was only 15 minutes. Also I could see an advantage in getting a 6:30am service out there across peoples' feed early Sunday morning purely for its own sake, and also as a promotional for the 10am service.

So as you might imagine, after seeing such a good response to posting a 6:30am service, I decided we would continue to have the Sunrise Service every Sunday since it has continued to gain an audience. For example, these days our Sunrise Service averages around 10,000 views a week whereas *Worship From Home* gets around 20,000 views each week. So it really helps in sharing the message that we share two different styles of service on Sunday morning.

In fact, I'd be happy to do it every morning except that it wouldn't be fair to ask Ezekiel to get up and dressed that early every day and who's to say that people would be interested in something like that besides on Sunday. That being said, after we saw our numbers grow from 2200 Palm Sunday to 7500 total views Easter Sunday I questioned whether we would ever reach that many again or if that was merely an anomaly of it being Easter Sunday. This year Easter was a snowy day in Denver and everyone was under coronavirus stay-at-home order with nothing else to do. So I thought, surely something like this is an anomaly, surely there's no way it will ever happen again.

However, and somewhat miraculously, what we've seen Sunday after Sunday is a growing and growing response to our sharing the message. For the fact is that all this has been quite a ride these past few months since it all began. And one of the most significant changes we've experienced is we've all become small-time televangelists overnight! Because when we first started *Worship From Home*, we had never made much of an effort to put ourselves out there. Yet once we saw how people responded to our simple efforts of sharing the message online it just inspired us to share it more often, both in word and in song.

This speaks to something I've been learning about myself over the past few months. I didn't realize, but before COVID-19 I had actually inhibited myself from reaching out to a larger audience. And what I am learning is that I never took seriously the opportunity to use technology because of what I thought of as modesty, but what was probably really rooted in a fear of putting myself out there. For all of these years I've been happy just speaking and singing and sharing my gifts with a small congregation behind the walls of a church building, yet for some reason I'd never even attempted to address an audience outside of the building.

However, once we were forced by the stay-at-home orders to share the message online we have since seen such an extraordinarily miraculous response over the past few months that now I can't help but believe that this is the direction God wants us to go. So after all these years of serving as a local church pastor, why did it take a pandemic for me to recognize that I was being called to share the message of Jesus beyond the walls of the church building?

It reminds me of Jesus' Parable of the Talents in Matthew 25, where the servant who received just one talent went and buried his talent in the ground. Why? Because he was afraid. Remember how, when the master came and asked him why he didn't invest his talent the man made the excuse that "I was afraid and so I hid your talent in the ground" (Matthew 25:25). In fact, 25 years ago, as a young preacher in my first church, I remember how I hated that verse because I felt like it's not fair to the one-talent guy.

So how ironic, I thought, that now 25 years later in my ministry that this message comes to us from Matthew chapter 25 verse 25! Because here today, right now in this moment, I am hearing this verse as speaking directly to me and saying to me that "So far, Canaan, you've been burying your one talent in the ground because you've been afraid!"

For that's where I've been stuck, in fact you might say I've been stuck in this same rut for 25 years, which is that I've only been practicing the art of ministry inside the walls of the church building rather than outside its walls, as Jesus commanded us to do. Again Jesus said "Go ye therefore and make disciples of all nations" (Matthew 28:18-20), he never said "Sit behind the walls of a building and call it a church"!

Consequently, I've had a rude awakening in this time and a conviction that the reason I haven't been putting myself out there until this point is because I was afraid, and not on account of any false modesty or whatever has been my excuse for hiding God's light under a bushel all this time. For as Jesus said, "You are the light of the world. ... No one after lighting a lamp puts it under a bushel basket, but on a lamp stand so it can give light to all the house. In the same way, let your light shine before others ..." (Matthew 5:15-16).

Another breakthrough I've had recently in regards to Jesus' command to "Let your light shine" came through my study of *The Big Book* of Alcoholics Anonymous. For while Christians in recovery often refer to the Bible as the Bigger Book, all A.A.'s consider *The Big Book* to be our primary sacred text in regards to any questions about alcoholism.

Anyway, one morning during my 7am meeting, someone mentioned a particular passage from page 164, which is a very well-known passage because it's considered the last page of the authorized part of *The Big Book*. However somehow the way they put it struck a particular note in me that day and ever after it's seemed like I've come unstuck in regards to how God is providing inspiration and how I'm supposed to recognize it and follow up on it productively.

As it says on page 164, "God will constantly disclose more to you and to us. Ask Him in your morning meditation what you can do each day for the man who is still sick. The answers will come if your own house is in order". Hearing this passage again that day, somehow I was struck by the idea that, if I was sincere in seeking God's will and asking how I can be of service, then all the inspiration I am constantly being given around various projects - writing, music, business ventures, mission opportunities, etc. - must be messages from God representing God's will for my life.

And while that might not seem like a revelation to some, for me as a person who has always struggled with the inner critic, the voice inside telling me it's not good enough, it was a liberation. For to my mind I was finally being granted permission to move forward with my creative projects. The result was like a dam burst open. Because I'm the type of person who has scads of notebooks filled with ideas - two different books I've been working on for years, not to mentions dozens of songs I've written and even recorded - all of which I just do for myself personally and never share with anyone else. I'm just too self-critical. But having had this experience over quarantine of really having no choice but to put myself out there, and now having this flash of insight from the passage in *The Big Book* that suggests these ideas are actually inspired by God, I started to consider that maybe I should share these things with the larger world.

That's why I believe it took God forcing the issue of putting myself out there through this quarantine, something totally out of my hands, because if it had been up to me I would probably have been perfectly comfortable just doing the same thing I've done for the past 25 years. Not to say I'm really doing anything differently than I was inside the walls of the church, rather the difference is in those I intend to receive it: people "out there" rather than people "in here".

It's not like it's entirely up to me, either, because there's a lot of pressure in the established church around tradition, or in other words, "We've never done it like that before!" That's why, for pastors, there is an expectation to direct their message to those gathered in the pews on Sundays. Since those same people pay the pastor's salary, it's almost impossible to make a case for doing things any differently.

So for me, that's one of the big take-aways that I've gained from this season, which is that if we had not been forced into the situation of expanding our audience by changing our channels of communication then we might never have made that shift, because the forces maintaining the status quo are just too difficult to overcome. But now that the pandemic has forced us to pivot towards a new way of communicating, the immediate results we've seen only prove what we are doing now is quantifiably better than what we were doing before: that is if our objective is truly to follow Jesus' command to make disciples of all nations.

In order to make this shift, however, we had to let go of things like our perfectionism and of taking ourselves so seriously that get in the way of the message. That's the mistake it seems a lot of churches are making by basically replicating what they were doing before on Sundays but directing it online, whether with an individual priest going through her prayer book, or with an elaborate broadcast ministry set-up. For no one wants to watch anyone trying too hard, it comes across as insincere or makes the viewer uncomfortable. So why are some of these communicating, while others are not? It is only by the grace of God.

That's another reason why I've appreciated a chance to do something different, because prior to COVID-19 I would spend my Saturdays writing sermons for Sunday. Yet ever since we started *Worship From Home*, I've chosen not to spend any time preparing a manuscript sermon because I can't imagine how it would ever connect effectively online. Instead Niki and I started that first *Worship From Home* service by having a conversation and it got such a good response that we've continued the format to this day. And what that means is that I now spend my Saturdays doing what I want - spending time with the family or working on the house - and save my writing for projects like this book.

At first it was a challenge, because being used to such a hectic schedule day-after-day, up and out the door by 6:30am, once we went on stay-at-home orders I still felt the need to get established on a regular routine. Both of our kids get up by 7am no matter what, and they always go to bed by 9pm. But now that they are no longer going to school in the morning they tend to sit around the house watching YouTube and playing video games. Consequently, that first week of quarantine I made up a calendar where I scheduled every hour around activities and music practice and reading and all kinds of things for the kids to do. The kids fought me on these things again and again, however, so after a few days I decided to let it go. Fortunately my attitude has gotten less and less rigid as time goes on, and in the process I learned to let go of what would be my expectations in normal times. Despite all my best laid plans, what happened is that the experience took on its own organic shape, especially after Peggy died, and slowly but surely we all started to adapt to a new normal.

Which brings up another thing that I've really appreciated about this time of social-distancing. I've picked up my guitar again after years and years of just leaving my beautiful Martin HD-35 acoustic sitting in a case in my office except for worship Sunday mornings between 9-11:30am. Because as much as I love the guitar - for instance, I bought my first guitar with the money I earned on my paper route when I was just 14 years old - recently I had fallen into a bad habit of not playing except when I was "working". And sadly, other than that I never picked up the guitar at all.

One of the first things I did when I started working from home is to set up my home office in the basement where I have a rack of different guitars, basses, and banjos lining the walls. For although I play all these instruments and have great examples of each, it was the rare occasion that I would even take one off the wall or out of its case and noodle around on it. Under quarantine, however, hardly a day's gone by that I haven't put my hands on a guitar or a banjo or another instrument for at least half-an-hour.

Not only am I playing all my instruments again, I'm actually doing more creative projects all the way around and the rest of the family is, too. That's what a friend of mine who's a songwriter says has kept him sane during this pandemic - what he calls "creative projects in my room" - and I agree with him that those of us artist types who've taken on these kinds of creative projects in our rooms have a hedge against purposelessness that most people don't seem to have.

Actually, if I had kept a diary of all the different creative projects we have done during this time I would first list my song, "Quarantine," I wrote that first week after we went under stay at home orders. Here's an sample verse: "Holed up indoors they call it stay-in-place/ But sitting here it feels like quarantine/ Stock market down, folks have lost their jobs/ Wondering if the cure's worse than the disease/ They say Kenny Rogers knew when to fold 'em, but for me, I don't have that luxury/ Instead wake me up when it's all over/ cause I'm already bored of quarantine." Just sing the lyrics to the melody of "Does Fort Worth Ever Cross Your Mind" by George Strait and you'll hear what it sounds like!

This was around the middle of March, right after Kenny Rogers died, which is why I mention him, and as I said, I hadn't picked up my guitar in years. But after a couple of weeks of stay-in-place orders I had all kinds of creative ideas running around in my head. So I took this song idea and ran with it - even recorded a video of my singing it sometime late in March - but then chose not to do anything more with it, probably because after Peggy died my attention was focused on the ministry 100%.

Speaking of songwriting, to be fair I would also have to recall our other song named "Quarantine," however this one was a parody of the ABBA song "Dancing Queen" that we wrote collaboratively together as a family. It was a particularly memorable event because all of us contributed to the lyrics and then we choreographed it and performed it for the church talent show Sunday night on Zoom.

Yet for me, this version of "Quarantine" was notable not only as a good memory of our time together, but also as a marker of how comfortable I had become with just doing a silly skit on camera, something I imagine that I never would have done prior to the quarantine era. For while before the pandemic, I would have made all kinds of excuses not to do a Facebook video, now that we're under the circumstances in which there's really no other possible way for us to communicate, I am finally learning to put myself out there.

9

However strange it might seem, one of the most fascinating lessons of this quarantine has given me a tremendous metaphor for what we've all experienced in our culture over the past several months. This was the saga we had this summer with our lawn and the fairy ring. And again, to tell the story I need to go back to the summer of 2018, the summer when we first had people staying in our house for five weeks responsible for watering our lawn.

For after the events of that spring, I had arranged to take a months vacation at my mom's house in Florida to chill out. However, returning home, we were met with a bare patch in the front lawn in the shape of a rainbow, about 30 feet long by 6 feet wide. We wondered what had gone wrong, but afterwards we just covered it over using an insta-sod type application I learned from a lawn-maintenance guy.

The lawn stayed nice and green all through the next year. Yet when our grass started growing back this spring, just as the quarantine was being announced, we noticed that the rainbow-shaped bare patch was back and even larger this time. So we began checking into it and realized that just underneath the soil was a whole lot of white powdery chunky mycelium looking stuff. It was then that I recalled how we had had mushrooms growing in that same rainbow pattern over the past couple years and thought it was strange, but never considered what might be lying beneath the soil to cause it to happen. Still it didn't take much effort turning the soil to uncover the fact that down about 2 inches deep, less in some places, there was a 30ft. x 10ft. wide rainbow-shaped patch of mycelium under the soil.

After I started digging, I realized the extent of it and called on three degreed experts to give us advice: two lawn and tree companies and one large nursery. Unfortunately because of the quarantine the state agriculture office was closed so I wasn't able to get a soil sample. However the two experts that visited on site told me they'd never seen anything like it. One suggested to just keep remedying the soil in hopes it would go away. The next one recommended pretty much the opposite solution: digging it out 3 feet deeper and 3 feet wider on either side and replacing it with brand new clean soil. He was the first person to apply the name fairy ring to what we were dealing with, though he said he had never seen one close to as large as ours. So because I got different opinions from the first two experts I reached out to a third expert, the tree doctor at one of the larger nurseries in the area, who said it should be okay just to remedy the soil with a lot of compost and then reseed.

Afterwards I researched fairy rings and discovered this was something that happened all through history and there's a lot of myth attached to it. For example, some say that fairy rings are a sign of luck and that to disturb one is bad luck. My son especially has gotten a lot of entertainment out of this idea that the fairy ring represents some sort of ancient mystic phenomenon that's taken up residence in our lawn.

Plus all this was happening under the canopy of an almost seventy-year-old locust tree that dominates our front yard. That meant that we couldn't bring in any heavy equipment on account of not wanting to damage the root system. So after all that research on fairy rings, both from the experts and from what we learned on our own, we finally decided to do kind of a combination of what they told us. Which meant we planned to dig it all up and then remove as much mycelium as was reasonable and replace it with new soil.

First we hired a man with an aerator to go over it a dozen times, about a half-hour job. Next we hired someone with a tiller and the guy spent probably two hours with his huge heavy tiller digging up the front lawn. Now that was a job! But although everything was tilled maybe 6 inches deep all the way through it still wasn't deep enough, for it had only scratched the surface of all the fungus that was underneath.

Because we couldn't use heavy equipment we went in with forks and shovels and dug down about eighteen-inches deep. We dug it all up, turned it all over, and then took all the excess sod that the tiller tore up along with some of the chunkier pieces of mycelium and stuffed it all in huge black Hefty bags. We filled about 30 of them, then afterwards we lined up six of the bags besides the garbage can. Niki tells me how she watched as the garbage man threw away four of the bags then tried to lift the fifth one and just shook his head, got back in his truck, and left. Afterwards we put one or two in the trash bin every week until they were gone.

To replace it, we brought in four or five loads of compost as well as topsoil. The back of my Volkswagen, I discovered, can carry 20 to 30 bags of a cubic foot apiece. So I brought the compost home and the whole family joined in together to mix 50 bags of compost into the ground with pitch forks and shovels over three different applications. Afterwards we mixed up an additional 30 bags of topsoil, mixing it with Kentucky blue grass in the insta-sod formula I learned from the landscaper earlier. We did it with the insta-sod not only because it's cheaper but because in my experience it's more permanent than sod even though it takes some time to grow. All of this took several days and I was particularly glad we had our 15-year-old son to help.

Speaking of Ezekiel's help, as soon as we had some warm days we tore out the stumps of the old pfitzer bushes I'd had removed from the front of the house probably a year and a half ago. They came out way easier than I expected, and although I had considered using chemicals to remove them ultimately I just busted them up with a pickax and then pulled them out by the roots. Ezekiel and I had been doing so much rock-climbing until this quarantine we were probably as strong as we've ever been at that time, though it still gave us sore backs for a couple of days afterwards.

It was also Ezekiel's idea to take some of the small boulders and big rocks buried willy-nilly amongst the gravel and set them up as a ring around the front garden. Inside the rock ring we built three garden boxes out of cedar fence slats where we planted Colorado wildflowers. All of this project took place simultaneous with the work on our front lawn, because we figured if we were fixing the lawn we might as well finish up the front garden so that it also looks good.

So it was that about a week from when we spread the insta-sod, there was already enough green on it that you could tell we were growing grass. Another week later and the new green grass was as tall as the darker green old grass that surrounded it. It was amazing. "It's like we're seeing a Discovery Channel documentary or something!" remarked one passerby. One day, maybe three weeks after we planted we got seven compliments from seven consecutive passers-by right in a row! And still to this day, whenever we are working in the front yard inevitably someone walking or driving by will comment on how great our grass looks.

One couple, neighbors we had never met before, even knocked on our door to ask how we did it. They shared how they had tried to re-sod their property and months later they said it still didn't look as good as our grass did after two weeks. We continued to let it grow for about a month before we first mowed it - watering every day - and now we have the thickest front lawn on the block.

But again, the reason I tell this story is because, for me, it was a direct analog to our experience as a nation with the COVID-19 pandemic. Because as I said, it's been around a year-and-a-half since we first saw the rainbow shaped dead patch in our lawn after we returned from Florida. However at the time, I wasn't really interested in actually diagnosing and getting to the bottom of the underlying problem.

Instead I was happy just to put a Band-Aid type solution on it in the form of the insta-sod application which made the grass pretty again for a season. However, as I discovered this spring, my insta-sod solution only papered over the problem, and this year it came back worse than before.

And no doubt there's a clear analogy here to so much of what we are learning about ourselves during this time of coronavirus: about our vulnerabilities, about the cost of doing business, about racism, greed, abuse of power, deceit, and all the ugly motives that now corrupt the basic institutions of our culture. All these things, it seems, are coming to light and being exposed in such a time as this. For as the scripture says, "For we do not wrestle against flesh and blood, but against the rulers and authorities, the cosmic powers of this present darkness, and the spiritual forces of evil in the heavenly places" (Ephesians 6:12).

So it is that I see a connection between some of the things we are literally digging up at our house now that we are spending so much more time at home, and all the things that are even now being dug up in our culture because we hit the pause button for awhile and people started paying attention. For in these times it seems we are starting to pay attention not only to how things appear on the surface but digging down even deeper still to some of the underlying concerns. These are things we might not have seen under normal circumstances, or things we did not see or passed over or chose to ignore, or things that were for a long time lying undetected, but which our situation in these times is finally allowing us to uncover and bring to the surface.

This is why, after months of quarantine, the attention of the world was captured by the horrible death of George Floyd by a police officer in Minnesota. Floyd's gruesome murder was a 10 minute lynching of a handcuffed man by an officer who sneered and smirked on video while he did it. The callous attitude of the officer towards his life - caught on tape by a bystander - made Floyd a martyr for our time.

Floyd's death first caught my attention because he was a Christian, active in his church in Houston where he was part of a vocational rehabilitation program that brought him to Minneapolis. What's more, his words "I can't breathe" while the policeman knelt on his neck recall Jesus' words from the cross "I am thirsty" (John 19:28).

Indeed, it may be that 2020 is event horizon for America. For with a resurgence of coronavirus outbreaks as a result of the lack of observing social distancing measures, people suffering economic hardship from job loss, and anger about police brutality and racism, all these factors together create the perfect storm for the presidential election in November.

Plague, financial insecurity, violence, protests, and from the way it appears things are only getting worse. Yet in the midst of all of this chaos and uncertainty, the church has an unprecedented opportunity to be a force for peace and love and good in the world. For in an era where people are increasingly coming to understand that the emperor wears no clothes, it's up to the church to cast a narrative that is noticeably different than that of the temporal authorities.

Recall how the church was founded upon a scenario much like this one with George Floyd, where a man was unjustly killed by the government in a manner that commanded the attention of the masses. Today however, the power of social media to broadcast events immediately all over the world allows an event like this to impact people - even to change the world - potentially in a matter of days rather than years.

Back to the analogy of the fungus in my yard, again the point is it was there all the time and when it first cropped up a couple years ago I just put a Band-Aid solution on it with the insta-sod and it worked for a season. But the next season, when it came back worse than ever, for a minute I was tempted just to cover it over again like I had before. This time however, I tried to get to the root of the problem, getting expert opinions in addition to my own research which led me to dig out the bad soil and mix in 50 bags of compost to remedy the soil before planting new grass.

Yet the fact is that if it had not been for the coronavirus quarantine I don't know that I would have had the patience to even do the research on what was going on with my lawn not to mention taking all the painstaking, time-consuming steps it took to get to the root of the problem. During this time of pandemic, however, when we finally saw the extent of the damage, we knew we had to do something even if we had to dig all the mycelium out and turn under new soil.

Of course, all this is an analogy to the times in which we live when we're finally giving attention to what lies beneath the surface. Maybe it's because we normally have such a short attention span, or because we're so busy with the rat-race, or since we have so much else going on, but although all the tools were available before we weren't using them.

Instead the event horizon of this pandemic had to reach a boiling point, prompted by the video lynching of George Floyd and a police department that covered it all up until they were finally exposed. So many secrets and lies, it begs the question of how often it's happened before. And we all know it's not the first time either. Indeed, many of us have been about the work of trying to call attention to these questions of injustice for a long time already. "How long, LORD?" we ask (Habakkuk 1:2).

But this time it's different. For one thing everyone now has a phone capable of passing video back-and-forth instantly around the world. People can observe police misconduct and within hours receive millions of views by posting it on Facebook or Instagram or YouTube. Closed cases of police involved deaths similar to what happened to George Floyd - such as Elijah McCain in

Denver or Tony Timpa in Dallas - are now finally being brought out into the open. For while we're all of us avoiding being exposed to the coronavirus, at the same time everything else is being exposed to the light.

What's more, because our church is connecting with so many people more here and around the world right now, we are now having one-to-one conversations with people about these matters online where we hear the thoughts and opinions of people in places much different than here. And what I've heard from many of the folks I've talked to is sadness that the dream they've had of America as a land of freedom is perhaps not as realistic as they had hoped.

In particular, I hear a common theme from our contacts in Africa - in places like Ethiopia and Kenya and Uganda and Nigeria and the Congo - that could well be encapsulated in one person's comment on our church page on a post made In Memory of George Floyd. He said, "Black Lives won't matter until African lives matter!" And sadly, I must admit that I would never even have considered this perspective if not for the dialogue I'm now having with African Christians through the connections that our church is making online,.

Since then, however, I'm inquiring into what people are contending with in the places from where they are reaching out to our ministry online. And what I'm only beginning to learn is that some of the people we are connecting with live in countries where there is no such thing as freedom of religion or women's rights or children's rights or minority rights of any kind, places where terrible atrocities still happen so often that they could only dream of the freedom and security we take for granted in the United States.

You might say God is just turning up the volume louder and louder until we hear the message. But again, and like our finding the fairy ring underneath our front lawn, all this is only revealing what lies underneath the surface. So it is that this pandemic is allowing the powers and principalities to be exposed. Not that we didn't have evidence of these things before, but today these events are unfolding in such a way that we would have to be blind to say we do not see.

10

Over and over, we've heard it said that the primary difference between what we see happening today compared to what was happening yesterday is that the technology is now available to make public things that before had always been kept private. We've seen this theme often in the news lately, particularly in regards to exposing police brutality. Again, it's not that the brutality wasn't happening before just that it wasn't so easily documented.

By the same token, over the past several months of the COVID-19 pandemic you might say that our church has been making public what before was ostensibly private, and as a result we have been connecting to a much larger audience. For when we shifted our priority to sending our message out on Facebook or YouTube, for the first time we were directing our primary attention to others beside those who are gathered within the walls of the church sanctuary.

Of course, before COVID-19 we never really thought about it this way because it was just the way we had always done it. Not that I fault the churches or the pastors for not realizing that our focus was far too much on ourselves. Because for my part, over the past twenty-five years there's no doubt that the expectations of attending to the needs of the building, preparing a traditional sermon, and all of the other tasks associated with the established model of church consumed so much of my time and attention that I never really considered the option to do things differently.

But now that we are forced by the circumstances of this pandemic to find a different model, the idea of going back to the way things were almost seems silly. Just imagine, most churches spend dozens of hours and hundreds if not thousands of dollars every week to present a program of praise and worship that includes only whoever happens to show up inside the building. And if we share this with anyone outside the sanctuary it is an afterthought, at best.

In contrast, when we share our praise and worship in the virtual public square of the internet we are inviting untold numbers of people to participate instead of sharing our message with only a privileged few. Again, when I say privileged from my position as Senior Pastor of The Central Christian Church of Denver, what I mean is that it is truly a privilege to live in such close proximity to our facility on Cherry Creek South. For to live close enough to the most exclusive area of Denver that you can attend in person, to have transportation to get here, or to have time in your Sunday routine for grooming and preparation and travel and everything that is required to meet us in our sanctuary to attend a service of worship is undoubtedly a privilege.

Unfortunately, many people in this country seem to have considered church attendance as a right but not a privilege. That being said, without this pandemic and the resulting mandated church closures I imagine many churches and probably ours included would have just continued on doing the same thing we've been doing until we suffered our last gasp. Not that we were actively trying to ignore the people outside our walls, just that the expectations of doing things the way we've always done them before seemed so heavy.

COVID-19, however, changed that for the first time ever in history, or at least in my experience as a pastor. For the state's policy of closing churches by force of law as a matter of public health finally forced the church to take a break from "the way we've always done it before". This was an extraordinary circumstance because before this, in all of my 25 years of ministry, I've closed the church less times than I could count on one hand and always because of blizzard conditions bad enough to put people in danger.

That's just to say that the church being closed and worship services cancelled for any length of time is a circumstance we've never considered before. But regardless of whether or not it was intended to harm the church, as some people seem to believe, in my considered opinion and experience it has been an unqualified good for churches like ours that were operating without a break for, in our case, 147 years.

Maybe the church just needed a sabbatical. For what we found is that merely by shifting our attention outside the walls rather than inside the walls of the building - just by sharing the message of Jesus out in the virtual public square rather than sequestered behind the walls of our cherished building - we've already connected with many thousands of times more people than ever before.

That's why I had to chuckle when I saw an article in *The Onion* a few weeks ago titled "Biden Campaign Considers Using the Internet to Attract Voters" (5/06/20). Because of course the premise behind this article is that Biden is so old and out-of-touch that using the internet to attract voters is a new idea for him, which is a ridiculous premise, that's why it's fake news in *The Onion*. But it made me laugh, because in my experience it quite accurately describes the attitude of many churches towards engaging with new technology.

For with 2.6 billion active users, far more than any other active constituency group in the world, today Facebook is undoubtedly the new public square, and as a result it seems like it's an important place for the church to be. For as the most prolific and accessible free social media platform and interface between individuals in the world today, Facebook portends the future hope and possibility of a place where people are no longer separated from knowing each other by either geographic distance, ability, or economic status.

What's more, it's not limited even to your own city or state or nation. That's why whenever I hear people calling for our government to nationalize Facebook it comes across not as beneficent but as xenophobic, because clearly the vast majority of the 2.6 billion people on Facebook are outside the United States! In addition, no matter where you are in the world we're all having the same experience since all 2.6 billion of us have the very same technology platform.

That was a huge revelation to me on our mission trip to Thailand in 2017 where I saw how people in that country, who had next to nothing materially compared to people in the United States, were able to find equal access in the area of technology. In fact, before that experience I was not a big fan of Facebook because from my perspective it seemed like people were now spending all their time taking selfies or pictures of what they had for dinner and sharing it with their friends. However, the fact is I've had a Facebook account myself since graduate school in 2005, so the only reason I scoff at it is because I have the privilege to do so.

Because what I've learned is that those of us who are blessed to have access to beautiful spaces - like our church building on Cherry Creek South, or the concert hall where we see symphony concerts, or even my son's orchestra room at his public school - can afford to scoff at venues like Facebook and other virtual spaces that may be the only opportunity people who don't have the same type of access we do can get connected. Consequently, and speaking as an admitted despiser of Facebook for many years, I've now come to believe it's an elitist sentiment to despise Facebook because Facebook provides free access to information to literally billions of people who have less access than myself.

In other words, today Facebook is the great equalizer. It puts the exact same tool in each person's hands here and around the world whether you live in India or the United States or whether you have Samsung or iPhone or Huawei. Of course, this is not true in China or other countries with totalitarian governments like North Korea. But with these exceptions Facebook now allows everyone to communicate on the same platform using a public voice that is potentially equivalent to everyone else's so that everyone has the same opportunity to exercise that voice in a virtual marketplace.

Facebook may be pointing the way towards the potential for international democratization on a scale like we've never seen just by establishing a platform where billions of people can communicate simultaneously. Because at this point in time, no other nation or entity - not China, not the United States, not the Catholic Church or Sunni Islam - can compare to the numbers who are connecting on Facebook.

What's more, most of us can say from our own experience that as a commodity Facebook adds tremendous value to people's lives. For if appreciation equals time invested, arguably Americans, who spend an average of an hour per day on Facebook, appreciate Facebook more than many of the other things we have, despite all of the luxuries that we enjoy here in the richest country in the world. For while the average American might have 100 times the income of the average Indonesian, for example, we both spend an hour a day engaging with the same social media platform!

That's just by way of recognition that by using Facebook we choose to participate in the most egalitarian marketplace of ideas of any in the world. For whenever we communicate in the virtual space, or gather in the virtual room, we are now more able to accommodate diversity, particularly economic diversity, than in any other space in the world. So as a church we are blessed to have even a small presence in this virtual space, and I believe we are remiss if we don't speak into the virtual

Facebook space just as we are called to speak out into the highways and byways (Luke 14:23).

Equally important, the potential we have to save costs through using the virtual room as opposed to the physical space is a moral issue, by my calculations. For by using the virtual rather than the physical space we have the potential to save thousands on the expenses inherent in maintaining physical structures where people can gather.

What's more, we could potentially save from using energy for heating and cooling the physical space and for transportation to and from that space that heretofore we believed was necessary for gathering the church. Plus if the church is able to gather more safely and effectively and provide more equal access in the virtual space than we can in the physical space, then it begs the question of why we are spending huge amounts of money to support church buildings that often sit empty and yet require ridiculous maintenance, heating and air-conditioning costs in order just to keep the doors open.

As I mentioned, our 60,000 square foot facility can seat 750 people in the main sanctuary and probably another 120 in the chapel, however our energy bills can be as much as $10,000 a month, not to mention the other maintenance and custodial costs it takes to run such a large facility in our part of the country. Other extraordinary expenditures, like the new roof we put on last year at a cost of $275,000, add still more to the cost. And it's not like we have a huge congregation with money to burn. Instead, because of the cost of maintaining our large building, we are grateful we can support our budget through a combination of both pledged contributions and income off of invested funds.

In contrast, imagine if the church held its largest gatherings in a virtual space then we wouldn't need to spend so much money maintaining our decaying properties which takes up the majority of our attention as pastor, staff and volunteers. So if this pandemic provides us an opportunity to recognize that all these structures that are established to preserve all of this property and all of the expenditure that it requires to fund these structures is maybe not the best use of our time talents and treasure, it might turn out to be a blessing.

In this way, the crisis becomes an opportunity, but only if we don't fight to resist the inevitable change and demand to go back to the old buggy-whip factory. For the truth is that God is trying to drag us kicking and screaming into the future. And from my perspective, God is trying to teach us that our current practices are unsustainable: that although we're keeping busy, we're not spending our time in healthy ways that add serenity, best value, and balance to our lives.

Not that there's no purpose for our buildings. For instance, some churches have beautiful architectural structures or historically significant properties that these congregations have made a commitment to maintain, and that can be a worthy and honorable vocation. Or perhaps the building provides a venue for performing arts, 12-step meetings, or other charitable or community work that appreciates our support. However, I argue that in order for a congregation to be a Biblical church they would also need to participate in some kind of worship or ministry that is outside of their interests in historic preservation. In other words, in order to be described as a church, a building should serve a larger purpose than just meeting its own needs (see Acts 2:42).

Again, I see a parallel happening here between the church and the rooms of recovery. Because from my experience as an old-timer in the church and the program of Alcoholics Anonymous, things are working out pretty well on Zoom. Actually, for people like me with long-term sobriety it's even better, because not only can we navigate the Zoom rooms we already have an established network of friends.

Still, we old-timers wonder about people trying to find the solution for the first time as our experience of connecting to communities of recovery were all via in-person contexts. In fact, a recent article titled "Alcoholics Anonymous, struggling to reach new members during the shut-down, expects a surge" (*The Washington Post*, June 12, 2020) reflects my concern that while people with long-term sobriety are finding Zoom meetings a satisfactory solution, newcomers may yet be having trouble getting connected.

That's why it's so fulfilling to see people like L. - not her real name - come into the Zoom rooms for the first time and get 90 days of continuous sobriety. She's been at the 7am Attitude Adjustment very day for the past three months and we've watched as she's put down the drink. To do this, she not only goes to the meeting, she's found a sponsor, reads *The Big Book*, does the steps, and is now carrying the message! So as someone who's been around for awhile, I can hardly express the gratitude I find in seeing someone like L. finding sobriety in the Zoom rooms for the first time.

In the same way, I've now had two men I sponsor call me up over this social-distancing time to tell me how new guys had asked them to sponsor them, which just goes to show that sponsorship is active and working in these times in the way it should work. For that's where the rubber really meets the road, when you start working with others, as we say in the program, and I was so glad these men had got to the point where someone saw in them something they wanted to emulate and that they had something to pass on. For there's a saying in recovery that "You can't give away what you don't have," which is why we wait for someone to ask us to sponsor them, and not the other way around.

In any case, the fact is the program of recovery is already working outside of the traditional in-person meeting rooms and I have plenty of personal anecdotal evidence from my own experience to say this with absolute confidence. So to my mind, this shows that the work of the church can also continue outside of our traditional spaces as well. Of course there are always some who refuse to try something new, whether it's in recovery or in the church, but as we've seen already over the past few months, even these people can ultimately connect when their need gets great enough.

Furthermore, at times it seems like people's refusal to connect online is really no more than just an excuse. Because from what I've seen, age is not a barrier to access. Many people aged 85 and older are actively participating in Zoom meetings or getting on Facebook as much as anyone else, both in recovery and in the church. And when seniors invite young people to help with technology it serves the dual purpose of building intergenerational relationships.

Still, it can be difficult, for some more than others. The other day, for example, I took a call from a woman I know in the program who told me that she was getting so lonely living by herself that she wanted to drink. Zoom meetings weren't doing it for her today, she said, and this is a person with long-term sobriety. So we talked on the phone, and afterwords she tells me how she asked her daughter to come sit with her for awhile -

social-distanced, of course - but as she put it, she just needed to lay her eyes on her.

Her frantic call reminded me that there are times when we all just need that direct interface of eyeball-to-eyeball or even skin-to-skin. Of course, I'm fortunate to live in a house with my wife and two kids and two dogs, so face-to-face contact isn't something I have the opportunity to miss. But people who live alone are in a much different circumstance and there's something about face-to-face human contact for which the screen is not necessarily a sufficient substitute.

Consequently, as soon as it's deemed safe, we will need to find some way to provide opportunities for people to connect in person periodically. The problem is the very people who most need to connect with others face-to-face are also the most vulnerable to COVID-19 infection. So we are still working out the details, recognizing we have a responsibility as leaders not to invite people into situations that present an undue risk to public health.

One model we are in the process of developing is the house church meeting, where small groups of no more than 12 gather together in individual homes around the metro area for worship, study and fellowship. Fortunately, we've done a lot of legwork on this plan already, so over the next few weeks we will be polling people's interest on how many would appreciate being part of a house church community.

Still, there's no denying that connecting via technology increases access for the overwhelming majority of people. Again, transportation is not required and technology is far less expensive than transportation, not to mention the costs associated with maintaining a physical room as compared to the nominal costs of maintaining a virtual space. In addition, and as we've discussed, technology greatly increases access for people who are differently-abled or who are geographically or economically isolated.

It's like my conversation with a lady in her seventies who at first needed a lot of coaching before she got connected to *Worship From Home*. Yet now she's learned how to get on Facebook we see her all the time, whereas we'd rarely see her at in-person church. "You have to admit, it's easier online, isn't it?" I asked. "Actually it's a whole lot better," she said. "Because now I don't have to get up so early!"

Not that the technologies weren't already available to do these things differently. The technology was already there, the difference is the crisis forced us to do things differently. So from what I've seen, the pandemic has done the church a great service because it forced us to take a long hard look at some of our practices that are ultimately unsustainable, and to finally recognize that there can be a better way.

11

Much earlier in the pandemic, sometime back in March as I recall, I read about a pastor - Satish Kumar of Calvary Temple, India - who said he had a dream like Joseph to store food for the troubles that were to come. Since then, their church has distributed more than 3.5 million meals to the hungry, giving freely to those in need, no matter whether they're Christian, Hindu or Muslim.

Reading this I was convicted of just how much more we could do as a church, especially now that we aren't quite so focused on ourselves anymore. For the amazing thing about this *Worship From Home* model is that it brings us into one another's homes. Meaning that people around the world can see into our home and they see us there - warts and all - and then they reach out to us on Facebook, and some of them are quite literally living in mud huts in the two-thirds world. Yet because we all speak English and have smart phones, here on Facebook we can meet on equal footing.

For what's amazing to me is how Facebook not only allows us to communicate across the miles at no cost, but it's also a way to enter into the life of someone and even begin to discern who a person is. That's why companies look into the Facebook accounts of potential employees because there's often no better barometer of who someone really is compared to who they might be presenting themselves to be. And while people certainly misrepresent themselves on social-media, it's possible we can gauge someone's sincerity at least as well on Facebook than in-person - or at least better than in an in-person worship service or interview where they would just be putting their best foot forward - because online we get more of a big-picture perspective.

That being said, already the fruits of what we are doing online have so surpassed my expectations that it's almost like the disciples fishing all day with no luck until Jesus said "Cast your net on this side of the boat" (Luke 5:4-6). For here we are finally coming up with a whole mess of fish!

And we've only just begun: considering how we now get 30,000 and more views of our message each week from here and around the world while before we were reaching less than 200 people at our Sunday morning service. It is nothing short of a miracle, and already the lines between nation, culture and race are being crossed by our witness in a way they never have before. And this is the result of less than four months of focusing on broadcasting our message online in contrast to the old way of sitting behind our walls.

Meanwhile, everything is fine here at home and most of our members seem happy connecting online. Nevertheless, now that we are growing our online congregation, one of the big questions I hear from people in the small circle of leadership here at Central is, "Why aren't we asking these people joining us online for donations?" And I respond by saying that in my opinion it comes across as insincere to ask people for money who tune in from all over the world - many of whom probably only make a few dollars a day.

For the fact is that we, as relatively rich Americans, have many times more than what most of our *Worship From Home* participants have out in the world. Consequently I think it would actually be wrong - even immoral - to ask money of largely poor Christians around the world, many of whom live on pennies or are literally dying for lack of food in this pandemic. Because from what I see, when I look back on so many of those looking in on Facebook, I imagine that, from their perspective, they see in us people they perceive to have a lot, while they have only a little.

In any case, we have a leaders' conversation on Zoom every Tuesday morning that includes the officers of the church plus Niki and me, which is a meeting I've conducted every Tuesday since I became Senior Minister in

2012 and now under stay-at-home we just switched it over to Zoom. And this past Tuesday they again brought up the question of why we haven't considered asking people tuning in online for donations, so I reminded them how it's not something that I'm comfortable with and gave them the reasons why.

So I was glad to hear Jim, our church Treasurer, chime in to say he understands how, if we were to ask people for donations without specifying what the donations are for they would just question if their contributions were going to make our pastor rich, which is exactly why I've been hesitating to ask for donations thus far. For as the public face of the church, and the one who would be putting my hand out, as it were, to request donations, the last thing I would ever want to do is come across as self-interested.

Also, at that point Julia spoke up and asked what the church was doing about outreach in the time of pandemic. Julia is our Cabinet Secretary, former chair of our outreach ministries, and one of the most dear people I have ever known. And while we are always generous to those in the family of the church and certain needs in our community, we haven't had a World Outreach project in a long time, probably since our youth mission trip to Honduras in 2018.

Of course, there's a number of reasons we haven't taken on any new World Outreach projects - mainly because our church has been through a lot of challenges lately - but it got me thinking. What if God had allowed us to take a pause on any new World Outreach projects over the past year or so because we were being prepared to take on new mission priorities in the year 2020 and God didn't want us to be encumbered by any old priorities?

For as the scripture says "For I know the plans I have for you, declares the Lord, plans for welfare and not for evil, to give you a future and a hope" (Jeremiah 29:11). So it may be that God allowed us just to let that field lie fallow for a season until we heard a clear direction and a word from the Lord as to what's next.

Afterwards it got me thinking about what was the right answer, because now that thousands of people are coming across our ministry online it does seem an opportunity to help direct their hearts towards being Christ's hands and feet. However, I was glad that our leaders understood why I was hesitant to ask for donations from those connecting online until I could discern the right course of action.

For almost as soon as the stay-at-home orders began back in March, we started getting requests for help via Facebook Messenger as well as on our page from people here in Denver and around the world. Of course, we'd gotten these requests before, but just like the volume turned up on our viewership it turned up on these kinds of requests as well.

In fact, that very weekend before the meeting I had stayed up late Sunday night responding to requests coming in from people in places like Africa, many of whom said they have so little especially these days that even pennies would help. Of course, at this time I have to respond to say, "No we're not in a position to do that right now." But who's to say that God is not calling us into the future or that we may soon be able to help in the case of these individual needs?

Praying over this, I believe God directed me to consider James 2:15-16 where the scripture says: "Suppose a brother or a sister is without clothes and daily food. If one of you says to them, "Go in peace; keep warm and well fed," but does nothing for their physical needs, what good is it?" For as a person who is accustomed to working with a lot of alcoholics and addicts as my personal mission field, I tend to be very cautious about offering financial helps so as to not create relationships of dependency. But now that I am talking with people who are suffering, even starving, in other parts of the world during this pandemic I realize we are dealing with something entirely different. For it may be that we have a responsibility to be helping to meet these needs if we are to be a true church according to the Bible.

With all this on my heart, I reached out to my dad that afternoon after the meeting to ask for his discernment on this question. For not only does Dad share the same priorities that I do on both church and recovery, as the director of several mission organizations and non-profits he has a lot of experience working with Christians of different sects and denominations around the world. So after I laid out the situation of how our church is even now connecting with so many people around the world, he agreed that if God is giving us the opportunity to reach so many people with a message of hope then God is also presenting us with a responsibility to help meet their needs.

Dad then called to my attention how many organizations that are intended to address hunger and poverty are either famously corrupt at the administrative level or how the money and supplies intended for help often never make it to those in need because of government corruption in the nations where the help is directed. This jibes with what I've heard from friends who are originally from countries in the two-thirds world, that aid from international missions organizations rarely trickles down to the people on the ground and so the best way to help is to somehow get the aid directly to the villages. In fact, we already have some experience working with people we know here in our local congregation who have family in other parts of the world in order to extend these kinds of helps directly.

Could it be that God was directing these thousands of people to connect with *Worship From Home* - including poor people from places in the two-thirds world like

Uganda and Thailand and Haiti - as an opportunity for rich Christians here in the United States to help to meet the need of poor Christians here and around the world? For through this technology that connects us one to another I can already see the potential for our church to do far more than what we are doing to help meet people's basic needs.

"Some of these people out there don't even have Bibles," Dad reminds me, suggesting that a major part of the work we're doing is providing a message of encouragement, strength and hope. "Just to get the message of Jesus out there is a huge gift," he said. "But there might also be a great benefit to some of your audience in providing online education free of charge because many people in the world don't have a lot of resources that here we take for granted."

Dad has a lot of experience in these things - for instance, he tells me how he is currently working with a Nigerian bishop to train and credential 800 pastors. Plus the reason our congregation has ordained more ministers than any other comparable church of our brand over the past few years is in part because of the high-quality, low-cost education he's provided for our ministers-in-training.

Already I'm hearing from people here and around the world asking if we have a branch of our church in their state or their country and I have to say, "No, but thanks for tuning in and they respond back to say, "Maybe one day you might consider it?" So I wondered, could this be an opportunity for *Worship From Home* to empower new ministers as Timothys and Priscillas of our church and to expand our brand beyond Colorado and around the world?

What's more, dozens of people from all over are writing to ask to receive Christ or if they can join the church online. Imagine a future in which we used this technology to train up people of good-will to be our accredited ministers and representatives in different parts of the world so that we can then direct people to our campuses in places like Florida or Mississippi, or even Uganda or the Philippines!

This was the concept Dad and I dreamed up in our hour-long conversation that day: for when we started talking about mission and education we started to imagine how to establish certain mechanisms of accountability between mission partners. Which goes back to the very issue of why I had been so hesitant to ask for donations thus far, because I wanted to make sure there was full transparency and there can't be transparency without accountability. Since then I have been working on developing relationships online with certain people in parts of the world where there already seems to be a lot of interest in our ministry.

Specifically I am attracted to people that have presented needs on behalf of others rather than those who just ask for something for themselves. Some are pastors or leaders already in their community, however thus far I've had to respond to most people's requests to say how we are currently overwhelmed by the need and have no scholarships or financial assistance available at this time.

Meanwhile, I am exploring the best methods of extending funds directly from the United States and making sure these transactions would operate under proper accountability. In the past we've transferred funds directly from our bank account, however we are learning more about apps like Venmo and others that can transfer donations instantly to individuals without regard for geographical proximity or other traditional barriers. So it seems the stage is even now being set for an outreach ministry that transfers small donations from Western Christians to Christians in the two-thirds world, vetting these needs and transactions through a system of accountability established through online membership in the church and virtual seminary training.

Towards this effort, we would provide teaching resources for free on our website as well as sponsoring mission work. This is what it would take to establish a ministry that could get education, food and necessities directly to the people in greatest need. Right now we're calling it Daily Bread - after the scripture from James 2:15-16 that I mentioned - although we've just kind of penciled in that name for now.

To get things started, I requested donations from a handful of people in the local community. At the same time I'm considering requests from people who've responded to our *Worship From Home* ministry. When something catches my attention then I'll follow up and take it one step at a time.

And while I have plenty of experience discerning between true and false in face-to-face encounters, at the same time to relate to people entirely online rather than in-person presents its own challenges. So I'm taking it slow, working with a few individuals to build relationships around mission projects, working with donors to help prime the pump, and then working with the treasurer to set up a specified account for donations going in and out. Eventually I hope to set up an automatic donation button online but for now we are handling each transaction on an individual basis.

For instance, one of the places we are helping is to support a family in Uganda who adopted a baby from a homeless woman who died of AIDS. The mother has her own newborn already and is struggling to feed the adopted baby she's now taken to her breast. She makes her living gleaning in the field and has barely enough to eat as it is, particularly in this time of COVID-19. A man in her village who has been following our *Worship From Home* program is who first brought the need to our attention. "Just 20 shillings for milk could keep this baby alive," he shared.

We started to build a relationship online, talked on the phone a few times, then partnered together to build a house of bricks for this family to replace their house of straw. Finding this project a success, we pray for what else we might accomplish here. I joked with our leadership team that the project reminds me of The Three Little Pigs because the upgrade from a straw house to a brick house is such a basic improvement to a person's situation. So it's awesome to be of help in making this kind of a difference.

In addition, our partner in this project is now working directly with my dad to establish ministry credentials so that we can establish some mechanisms of accountability with the goal of starting a mission branch of our church in Uganda. All this has happened with just the past six weeks or so, but we believe this project and others are a great start for this new idea in ministry we call Daily Bread.

In fact, it may be that by building partnerships in ministry with some of those who are connecting to *Worship From Home*, our church can find an opportunity to help create a way to meet the needs of "the least of these" (Matthew 25:40) that can transcend some of the obstacles larger aid organizations will founder upon. For our hope is that by starting partnerships with a few pastors in different parts of the world we can better meet the people's needs directly precisely because we don't rely on a heavy infrastructure.

Of course, the point is not only to build relationships with real people on the ground that we then empower to meet the needs of those who are without daily bread, but also to give people here in the United States the joy of being able to help others in the name of Christ. Yet most importantly, by working to help those who are "naked and without daily food" we are working to do what God requires of us to do.

Indeed, I believe that if we focus on how our church can help meet the needs of "the least of these" by sharing a message of hope and salvation with a hurting world then we can trust in people's generosity to naturally underwrite the other areas of our ministry. In any case, if we're already making these kinds of connections after just four months of *Worship From Home*, and we continue to follow in God's way, who knows where God may be calling us in the future?

12

Early afternoon on Tuesday, June 16th - totally out of the blue - I got another call from the prophet. "How's it going?" he asked. "You've been on my heart, so I'm checking in. And from what God's been showing me, it looks like He has been powerfully present in your life!"

By that point, it had been about three months since we started *Worship From Home*, and about a year-and-a half since we had last talked on the phone. What's more, it was now a little over three years since that first call I had from him where he gave me the prophecy to "hold your seat".

Also, that very morning we had buried one of the saints of the church, Ms. Mary, at 99 years old. It was our first in-person service in the church sanctuary since the pandemic. And Ms. Mary holds a special place in my heart because she played an extraordinary role in helping me first find my seat as Senior Minister of Central. So it seemed significant that the prophet was calling on the day of her funeral. What's more, at the very moment he called I was talking with a new friend from Uganda on the phone - the first voice call I had made on behalf of our Daily Bread ministry.

We talked awhile, just catching up, before I popped the question. "Not that it's any of my business," I said, "but from our experience lately it seems we might be on the cusp of something, maybe even the next reformation of the church. Could it be that God is calling us to a reformation where we are being asked to leave our buildings behind?"

"Exactly!" he said, without skipping a beat. "For the next era of the church is now upon us: the epoch of pure grace!" There was a high note in his voice and his pattern of speech changed. He then shared that we are entering the Last Days of prophecy. "Do you know Phyllis Tickle?" "You mean her theory that Christianity goes through a reformation every 500 years, and that we're now being de-institutionalized?"

"That's it," he said. "In her book, *The Great Emergence*, she talks about the 500 year epochs of the church" (see Phyllis Tickle, *The Great Emergence: How Christianity is Changing and Why*. Baker, 2012). "Basically, the first 500 years was an era of pure grace, no institutions," he explained. "Whereas the second 500 years ...". "What Hauerwas called 'The Constantinian Captivity of the

Church' ..." I chimed in. "... was a combination of law and grace," he continued.

"Meaning that the gospel of grace was still present in the church - think of theologians like Augustine, for instance - yet it was now partnered with the institution of the Roman government. That was the second epoch. The third epoch began when the Roman church split off from the Orthodox church around 1000 A.D. This is the period where the church was held entirely captive to the law, without grace."

"The fourth epoch began around 1500, with the Protestant Reformation and Anabaptist movements," he explained. "The gospel was still carried by institutions, but it started to break free of those constraints, particularly with the Pentecostal movements that began in the 20th century. So the past 500 years of the church, like the second 500 years, again represented a combination of law and grace".

"What Tickle argues," he continued," is that we are now entering the final 500 year epoch of the church, in which Christianity is becoming utterly de-institutionalized, meaning a return to the era of pure grace. But what this means is that all the forms of institutional Christianity will be stripped away: beginning with the icons of our heritage such as the statues that are now being torn down; then our church buildings and their tax-exempt status, where the church won't be able to afford to keep our buildings; and then, in the final stage, the very Bible itself will be banned."

"This is the final reformation," he said, "or what the Bible calls the Apocalypse, the Last Days. It was for such a time as this that we were called to hold our seats." He then told me some other things about the roles God is telling him we and our churches are supposed to play in the coming days.

Then it was like his voice shifted back into a lower register, and he seemed to relax a little. He told me how since we'd last talked on the phone a little over a year ago it had been an extraordinarily difficult time for them spiritually, but it resulted in their church being "purified so we are now only hearts that are true," as he put it. Of course, that would also be a perfect way to describe our experience over the past two years as well, with the same results, that we are now only hearts that are true. For like Gideon's army, God needed first to reduce us down to a faithful remnant so that we can stand to fight the battle that is to come (Judges 7:5).

Still one thing I've learned over the past two years is that a call from the prophet is not something to take for granted! And hearing how his experience so closely parallels mine gives me hope that we're doing the right thing. Yet I'm not a prophet - I'm more of an evangelist - so all of this is above my pay grade (see Ephesians 4:11).

Instead, I'm just grateful we're not too stuck in our ways to roll with the changes.

Later I thought of his words when I read a news story about a group of Catholics in St. Louis, Missouri who had been attacked trying to protect a statue of King Louis IX. Asked why they were protecting the statue, one woman called the statue "a religious symbol of everything I hold dear. I stand for him" she said. "But ultimately, I'm here for Christ the King!" ("Violent Protesters Punch Elderly Man, Attack Praying Catholics Who Were Protecting Louis IX Statue," Tre Goins-Phillips, *Faithwire*, CBN News, June 29, 2020). The story called to mind the words of the prophet, that "all of the icons and institutions will be stripped away," in order that we can learn how to be the church without any buildings, any forms, or even the Bible, but only grace.

"For the idols shall utterly pass away" (Isaiah 2:18). This is the promise of our God: that in the last days all the forms to which we cling so desperately will pass away so that we can become totally dependent upon God alone. "For on that day people will throw away … their idols of silver and gold which they made for themselves to worship" (Isaiah 2:2).

Isaiah's vision is expanded upon in the New Testament prophecy of Revelation, revealing God's ultimate promise: "But I saw no temple in the city, because the Lord God Almighty and the Lamb are its temple" (Revelation

21:22). Not to oversimplify, but the basic idea is that the "temple" is ultimately falling away so that God can transform each human heart. In fact, you might say this was the natural progression of the faith - towards de-institutionalization - ever since God tore the curtain of the temple in two at the very moment Jesus died on the cross. (see Matthew 27:51). For ultimately God's plan is for us to become free from attachment to anything besides the Holy Spirit, and for this to happen all the idols have to fall from their thrones.

That's why it's so important that we know the full promises of God as detailed in the prophetic books - from Isaiah to Revelation - because this gives us the perspective of eternity so that we don't have to be afraid. For when what I believe to be the inevitable events transpire in which the church will be disestablished from the culture, the Body of Christ on earth needs to know that this is not a reason to despair.

For at the same time, we will simultaneously experience a season of revival the likes of which we've only dreamed. Our own congregation, for example, already has the wind in its sails with an exponential increase in the number of people we are connecting with since we started *Worship From Home*. But I see evidence of it everywhere, like the posts I see on Facebook of people coming to Christ and miracles of healing happening on the very street corner where George Floyd was killed.

For again, God takes what was meant for evil and transforms it into something good.

In fact, knowing what we know now, and honestly, what we probably knew already only we were just afraid to admit it, would we really want to go back to the way things were? Still, it takes courage to face the fact that not going back - back to the days where we are all just "going" to church rather than "being" the church - is actually a good thing.

For my part, after the experience of *Worship From Home*, I believe it would be nothing short of selfish to return to the old model where we keep everything we have behind the walls of a building maintained exclusively for ourselves. For while we say everyone is welcome, in actual fact the only real way for someone to participate is if they have the resources to walk in the doors of their own accord, which in the first place means that they have to live at least in a certain proximity to our exclusive address on Cherry Creek.

All the while, the pastor and staff have their hands full taking care of more building than we have volunteers to look after and all the business-related headaches that come with it. For despite our best hopes and dreams for what the church could be, a pastor of a traditional denominational church model is so overwhelmed with expectations of "the way we've always done it before" that any time we have to attend to additional aspects of ministry is extraordinarily limited. For in my experience, the burden pastors carry just in standard expectations of running that model of business, particularly in a church like Central with a large building and a small staff, requires about a 60-hour work week.

Not that I'm blaming the pastors, for I know the burden of being a pastor as well as anyone. Neither am I blaming the congregation, who are just volunteers entrusted with the extraordinary responsibility of attending to something as ineffable as the Body of Christ. Yet when we say we want to "go back" to church, we need to be careful how it comes across. For are we saying that we, as privileged Christians in the United States - with our professional clergy and grand sanctuaries built by the investment of faithful generations before - would rather just maintain the status-quo?

This is the extraordinary privilege of being an American Christian, where as much as 20% of the population still attends worship services every week in these religious clubhouses established out of the priorities of a previous era. And I give thanks for these churches because this was a model that worked for generations, and we stand on the shoulders of all those who have gone before. Buildings like these were once the hubs of their communities, back before things like television, the internet, and Facebook.

However the culture just doesn't work that way anymore. For while a remnant of saints remain sheltered inside the church, oftentimes membership in these clubhouse-type organizations is more motivated by nostalgia than faith, and sadly many people go to church in order to control the institutional resources the church represents. In any case, if the old model serves anyone well it's only a privileged few.

That is why I am daring to state the elephant in the room, which is that I believe it would be a good thing if most of our churches never went back to that old model. What's more, from what I know as a church insider, I can say conclusively that it's delusional to think that we could ever really go back. For to be perfectly honest the clock is fast running down on that old model, and even the best endowed church probably has less than twenty years left to support their budget under the best of circumstances.

The point is that we can no longer live under the delusion that we can just go back to this old, unsustainable model. Even now we hear of churches that are deciding to shutter their doors permanently as a result of this pandemic. From what I hear anecdotally, between March 15 - June 28 more than 15% of all American churches made a decision to close.

The same is true of the clubs of recovery. For while it used to be that when you showed up to the York Street club any morning at 6:55am there were so many people there that the noise of laughter and conversation could be heard down the street. In contrast, now nearly four months after the start of the pandemic, whoever shows up to York Street at 6:55am has to flip on the lights of an empty dark room. Maybe a dozen people will join them over the next hour.

Meanwhile, every morning at 6:55am in the virtual Attitude Adjustment meeting we watch as 80, then 90, then 100, then up to 150 people check-in to the virtual room. And although we no longer have to park on the street and climb three flights of stairs, we are still greeted by the same friendly faces and welcome laughter. Sure, there can be challenges, but if we gain the same result - which is staying sober by the grace of God and the fellowship of Alcoholics Anonymous - it doesn't matter if it's virtually or in-person.

Prove me wrong, but I believe we have made this change permanently. For while people talk about how things will be back to normal after there is a vaccine, from what we see already I imagine that the longer this goes on, the less likely it is people will want to go back to the way things were. Because after, say, a year-and-a-half of adapting to the new normal, most people will come to see that there actually is an option to do most of the things we used to do for work and entertainment in a virtual space without the expense of travel and accommodations and without burning endless amounts of fossil fuel and we will recognize that there's no sense in spending all this money in this way. For what we will have learned over all those months of quarantine is there's a better purpose for all that money and a better, more balanced way for people to live.

In fact, could it be that this is the future hope God planned for us? For as the scripture says, "Then I saw a new heaven and a new earth ... the holy city, the new Jerusalem, coming down out of heaven. Its gates will never be shut by day and there will be no night there. People will bring into it the glory and honor of the nations" (Revelation 21:1-2, 25-26).

Looking closer, Revelation describes the city of God as being "built of jasper, while the city is pure gold, clear as glass" (21:18). What's more, the city has twelve "gates" described as "twelve pearls" (21:21). In description, this reminds me of what we see when we look at each other in a virtual space such as Facebook or a Zoom room in that we see a transparent shimmering screen - "clear as glass" - where different "gates" resembling shiny "pearls" allow us access to the virtual community. So perhaps John the Revelator saw a vision of the future city of God as a virtual meeting place and just described it the best he knew how?

Taking that premise for a start, it may be that a lot of other parallels can be made between the virtual space and the kingdom of heaven. For instance, the prophet

Isaiah anticipates a future hope where "the wolf will live with the lamb [and] they will not hurt or destroy on all my holy mountain" (Isaiah 11:6,9). So to continue the analogy, the virtual space can be a place for respectful dialogue where all participants can potentially have an equal voice, without regard to status or size or ability or geography or anything.

We've seen this happen in the virtual rooms of recovery, where some people seem to be able to share more freely from behind their screens. And what strikes me is that, just like the in-person rooms attempt to make no distinction between people on account of social or economic status, the virtual rooms are set up by design so that everyone has an equal portal and each person has the exact same access and presentation. When these rooms are appropriately moderated everyone can have an equal chance to share and dialogue respectfully, reminiscent of Isaiah's prophecy.

Or take for example, another of Isaiah's prophecies of the days to come where he writes, "Ho, everyone who thirsts come to the waters; and you that have no money come buy and eat!" (Isaiah 55:1). Again, could not this prophecy describe a time and a place where everyone is allowed equal access to a common technological platform that gives everyone a means for them to communicate without regard to questions of status or identity, like race, sex, nationality, ability, or orientation? Also, from what I understand the technology is available to erase the language barrier from these interactions, so that everyone can have equal access, whether you're in Haiti, Thailand, or the United States!

Of course, all of this is not to diminish the promise of the eschatological future hope we share of Jesus coming back at the end of time (see Revelation 19:11) but rather to draw a parallel between what's happening in our world today and the fulfillment of God's promises. For perhaps here we will discover that foretaste of glory divine in which the gospel can be lived out in a way in which more and more people will come to experience the blessings that many of us already enjoy in this life.

By this I mean that all the blessings of peace and security, the freedom to worship as we choose, food, shelter and clothing - a lot of the things we American Christians already have, yet still complain because we take it for granted - all of this freedom and security and prosperity will be available to everyone. So with that in mind, could it be that the Last Days are even now upon us? If so, our first job is to let go of our old ideas of "going back" to church - old delusional ideas, I might add - and instead embrace the change that's happening in the world right now as God's plan and purpose.

The saying "let go or be dragged" comes to mind, for from what I can tell this is not only an inevitable future but also potentially a more equitable future. This book is written as an embodiment of the hope that we will find the courage to walk boldly into this future, rather than to try and fight the change that God is forcing upon us through this pandemic.

For I don't know about you, but I choose to believe God is even now bringing us into a new way of life so that more space is available - virtually - for anyone who comes! For as the Scripture says, "Let us hold fast to the hope that we profess, for he who promised is faithful" (Hebrews 10:23).

Suyapa, Honduras, June 5, 2018

About the Author

Canaan Harris is Senior Minister of Central Christian Church of Denver (Disciples of Christ). He is married to his partner in ministry, Niki Jorgenson, and they have two children, Ezekiel and Eden.

www.ingramcontent.com/pod-product-compliance
Lightning Source LLC
Chambersburg PA
CBHW032035040426
42449CB00007B/895